Short Works of Octavius Winslow

Short Works of Octavius Winslow

NONE LIKE CHRIST

CHRIST'S SYMPATHY TO WEARY PILGRIMS

CONSIDER JESUS

BottomoftheHillPublishing.com

ISBN: 978-1-4837-0431-9

Content

NONE LIKE CHRIST

How is your beloved better than others?

Song of Solomon 5:9

The *power of contrast* is acknowledged by all. The **poet** studies it in the construction of his epic; the **artist** in the coloring of his picture; the **logician** in the arrangement of his argument; the **lover of nature** as his eye roves over the outspread landscape– all are conscious of the presence and power of this principle. The object of contrast is not to create the ideal, or to foster the fictitious; but to confirm the existence, and heighten the power and impression of the true. It is thus that the beautiful becomes more attractive, the grand more sublime, the good more excellent, and the object which awoke our admiration and inspired our regard, enthrones itself more firmly and supremely upon the soul.

The Word of God is replete with contrasts. In no volume is the effect more striking. How constantly, by an easy and graceful antithesis, the Holy Spirit places in contrast the vanity of idols, and the existence of God; the insignificance of man, and the greatness of Jehovah; the evanescence of things temporal, and the permanence of things eternal; the deformity of sin, and the beauty of holiness; the objects and attractions of earth, and the scenes and allurements of heaven; our waywardness and unworthiness, with God's mercy and love. With what power, beauty, and reality are the great things of God's word thus brought out!

In presenting to you, my reader, the Lord Jesus Christ, as worthy of your undivided affection, supreme confidence, and unreserved service, infinitely distancing and eclipsing all other beings and all other objects brought in competition with him, we purpose adopting this principle; assured that the result must be, with the accompanying blessing of the Holy Spirit, the supreme enthronement of Christ in your admiration, trust, and love, as the "chief among ten thousand, and the one altogether lovely one." Happy shall we be if the conviction of the truth is deepened in your soul, NONE LIKE CHRIST!

Nor could we engage your thoughts upon a subject more suitable to the new and solemn period of time upon which we have entered.

You are about to add another deathless chapter to the momentous volume of your personal history. As yet its lines are untraced, its events unrecorded. What that history may be, you have no vision to guide your knowledge; nor, if you are wise and trusting, do you wish to know– calm and fixed in the assurance that it is all prearranged in the covenant that is "ordered in all things, and sure," and that, impenetrable as is the veil that conceals it from your eye, God will permit nothing to transpire but what he has shaped and tinted with just that form and hue that will the most perfectly harmonize and blend, and will the most surely promote, your greatest well-being with his highest glory.

"What is your beloved more than another beloved?" It is clear, from this interrogation, addressed to the Church of Christ, that other and rival beings, other and competing objects, were brought into comparison with Christ, asking, if not a superior, yet an equal share of homage and regard; and the Church is challenged to a vindication of the higher and superior attractions claimed for her beloved Lord. "What is your beloved more than another beloved?"

It is a humiliating fact, that there exists no object, the most trivial and contemptible, which the unrenewed mind will not place in competition with, and choose in preference to, and delight in to the exclusion of the Lord Jesus Christ! Take a brief and summary view of these claimants to man's regard– these rivals of Christ– and see how far they are worthy of a moment's consideration, when brought in contrast with the incarnate Son of God. Before we proceed, however, to particularize, let us premise that this is no new phase or development of our depraved humanity. Our world has ever been a Christ-rejecting world. From the moment the angels' song broke in music upon the plains of Bethlehem, the prediction of the Christ-exalting prophet, Isaiah, commenced its sad fulfillment– "he is despised and rejected of men."

With some individuals, **SELF** is the rival– self in some of its many forms. Self-righteousness, self-seeking, self-indulgence, self-worship is the acknowledged and enthroned god– the "beloved" object of the unrenewed mind's supreme affection and worship.

With others, the **WORLD** is preferred to Christ– its acquisitions, opinions, and pleasures. O treacherous world what myriads have you drawn within your insatiable vortex, "drowning men's souls in perdition!" Reader, are you preferring its gayeties, its riches, its honors, its religion to Christ? Pause on the threshold of this solemn period of time, and ask– "What, should I die this year, will the world I have chosen in preference to the Savior do for me when eternity stares me in the face?"

Others place the **CREATURE** in competition with Christ; the creature and not the Savior is their "beloved." But what a fearful crime are they chargeable with, "who worship and serve the creature more (or rather) than the Creator, who is blessed forever." The creature is the defaced, the spoiled image of God. To prefer this marred and ruined temple to the glorious Being who constructed it, is to place yourself upon a level with the idolatrous Persian, who in his blindness worships the sun as the image of the Deity.

But what superior excellence and attraction has an earthly beloved, that you should choose, love, and adore it in preference to the Heavenly One, who, as human, is "fairer than the children of men," and who, as divine, is "God over all, blessed for evermore"? God will not hold him guiltless who loves, worships, and serves the creature rather than the Creator. Thus, there is nothing earthly, base, and contemptible which the natural man will not place above God, and prefer to Christ. His estate, his rank, his talents, his reputation, his very person, is "made to sit in the temple of God, showing itself that it is God," receiving the incense of adoration and worship, which alone belongs to Jehovah.

Reader, whatever earthly object reigns supreme in your mind and affections, dethrones and supplants the Lord Jesus. It may be your daily calling, or some pleasure of memory, or some object of taste– music, sculpture, painting, literature, science– whatever the master-passion of your soul, the supreme, all-engrossing object of your life, it is your Christ, your Savior, your beloved, your all; and with this, your only portion and preparation, you are, in a little while, to confront the bar of God "Where your treasure is, there will your heart be also."

But we approach yet closer our subject, and proceed to unfold the preeminent place Christ occupies in the universe of life, beauty, and love– in the world of nature and of grace– showing that there is not, amid this vast assemblage of magnificent objects and glorious beings, one like Christ.

"None like Christ!" How familiar is this sentiment to the family of God. Sometimes it is the expression of gladsome joy, at others, breathed in sadness and in grief. When some beam of holy rapture has lighted up the soul, and the preciousness of the Savior is felt, then the tongue exclaims, "None like Christ!"– there is no joy like that which Jesus inspires! Or, when some scheme of human happiness is blighted, some cherished friendship chilled, some idol-god smitten from its shrine, some earthly spring dried, turning from the scene, spirit-wounded, heart-saddened, and disappointed, the soul has fled anew to Christ, its true attraction and rest, and with a depth of emotion and an emphasis of expression, the inspiration only of such a feeling, the believer has exclaimed– "Lord, there is none like yourself! I learn your transcendent worth, I experience your matchless love, I behold your unrivaled beauty, I feel your inimitable tenderness, gentleness, and sympathy in this hour when my spirit is overwhelmed within me, and my earthly treasures float a scattered wreck upon the surging waters through which I come to you!"

But follow us, dear reader, while, in a, few particulars, we attempt to justify the preeminence of the Savior, and establish your believing soul in the truth that "there is none like Christ!"

I. No GLORY like His.

We begin with the statement, that there is no glory like Christ's glory. The universe is full of glory, because it is full of God. But God designed that his Son should occupy a place among created intelligences equal to himself touching his divinity, and inferior to himself only as touching his humanity; and both, mysteriously combined, constituting him "the head of all principalities and powers;" and, "that all men should honor the Son, even as they honor the Father," of whose glory Christ is the effulgence, and of whose substance Christ is the exact impress. The deep gloom of earth was never illumined with such a light as when the Son of God descended from heaven; and the brightness of heaven never shone forth with such a luster as when he returned back from earth, invested with the sinless robe of our nature– the divine prophet– the atoning priest– the triumphant king. Marvel not that all the hierarchies of heaven bend low before that central throne on which sits the glorified Redeemer, and that at his feet the elders cast their crowns. Surely, it is the wonder and the glory and hallelujah of heaven, that divinity could stoop so low, and not be less divine; and that humanity could rise so high, and not be less human. Oh! there is no glory like Christ's glory.

Reader, can you, with the exulting Evangelist, exclaim– "We have seen his glory, the glory of the only-begotten of the Father, full of grace and truth." Judge of the sacred vision by its hallowed effects– "We all, with open face beholding as in a glass the glory of the Lord, are *changed* into the same image from glory to glory, even as by the spirit of the Lord." This transforming, sanctifying influence of Christ's surpassing glory is real and palpable. One beam darting into your heart will pale the glory of the world, the glory of the creature, and the glory of self. And when this divine sun has risen resplendent on your soul– a child of darkness though you are– a worm of earth hiding in your obscurity and gloom– you may emerge from your cloistered solitude and woe, bask in its warmth, sun yourself in its effulgence, and exult that, as a pardoned sinner, a justified believer, an adopted child, all this glory of Christ's is yours– your robe of righteousness and your diadem of beauty– constituting you a king and a priest unto God.

Oh! rest not, beloved reader, until this divine light has come, and the glory of the Lord is risen upon you. Then, and not until then, will you arise and shine in the beauty of holiness, a child of the light, shedding its luster all around you; and henceforth, whatever be the leadings of your Savior, or the dealings of your God, the way along which he conducts you, checkered, winding, lonely, will be that of the "just, which is as the shining light which shines more and more unto the perfect day."

II. No BEAUTY like His.

Another observation naturally results from this– there is no beauty like Christ's beauty. We might expect that such divine glory, if ever it tabernacled on earth– the world's resplendent Shekinah– would be enshrined in a temple in all respects worthy of its dignity. We therefore find language like this– "When he comes into the world he says, sacrifice and offering you do not desire, but a body have you prepared me." It was a body prepared by the Holy Spirit, of real, yet sinless flesh, in which the Son of God was to dwell. Hence we find the inspired artist, in portraying Christ's beauty as man, represents him as "fairer than the children of men– grace is poured into your lips." Himself the source and author of all beauty, his own beauty eclipses all. We love to trace the creations of his beauty, in the varied and endless forms of loveliness which still linger, adorning and enriching this fallen world. Those bright constellations– Christ created them; those burning suns– Christ kindled them; those snow-wreathed Alps, those cloud-capped hills– Christ raised them; those verdant valleys– Christ spread them; that blushing rose, that graceful lily, that exquisite fern, that curious sea-flower tossed upon the shore, that wayside violet that screens the dew-drop from the sun, that winding stream, that leafy grove– Christ formed and penciled it all– Christ clad that magnificent landscape with its robe of living green; scented the air with its fragrance; and hollowed out the depth of that expanding ocean dimpled with beauty by the gentle breeze, or dreadful in its grandeur when trod by the giant storm. Truly, "he has made everything beautiful in his time." Oh! I delight to see the incarnate God, who died to save, scattering from the opulence of his own boundless resources all this jewelry, making man's sinful home so rich, so lovely, so attractive.

But his own beauty, who can describe it? His person so lovely, his nature so holy, his heart so fond, his spirit so gentle, his look so winning, his voice so soothing. His whole character, life, and demeanor so inlaid and resplendent with every human, spiritual, and divine perfection– truly, it was no imaginative picture, and it was no mere oriental imagery with which the Church, in her just and lofty conception, described him as the "Chief among ten thousand, and the altogether lovely one."

But Christ's beauty is shared with all those who have union with him. Washed in his blood, robed with his righteousness, and adorned with his graces, each believer is lovely, through his loveliness put upon him. And there is more of wonder, because there is more of God, there is more of beauty, because there is more of Christ, in that poor sinner who clings in penitence, faith, and love to the cross, looking up to God as a pardoned child, and pulsating with a life derived from the indwelling spirit, than in all this vast creation, enameled and sparkling with endless forms of loveliness.

Reader, has Christ's beauty caught your eye, and penetrated your soul, transforming you– reflecting his image in your Christ-like principles, your Christ-like spirit, your Christ-like walk, your whole Christ-like life? Then, dim and imperfect as is the copy, before long it will be complete, when you "shall see the King in his beauty," and join the faultless throng who encircle the throne of God and the Lamb. Oh! then, be it your employment to contemplate, study, and reflect the beauty of Christ, for there is no beauty like his!

"It is a finished portrait!" exclaimed an accomplished infidel, as the character of Christ was delineated to his view. It is a finished portrait– examine it, transfer it to yourself, and beware how you allow a creature's beauty– a being of human loveliness and love– to veil or shade a scintillation of Christ's surpassing beauty from your eye.

III. No LOVE like His.

There is no love like the love of Christ. The association of contrast will aid us here. God, who is love, is the author of all human affection. Love is the creation of Deity, the descendant of heaven, the reflection of God; and he whose soul is the most replete with divine love is the most like God. Paralyzed though our humanity is by the fall, tainted as it is by sin, the human heart is still the home of love in some of its loftiest and purest forms. It is impossible to behold its creations without the profoundest reverence. Who can stand, for instance, in the presence of a mother's love and not be awed by its dignity, won by its power, and melted by its tenderness?

But there is a love which equals, a love which excels, a love which surpasses it– it is the love of Christ! Institute your contrast. Select from among the different relations of life, the nearest and dearest; choose from those relations the deepest, purest, truest love that ever warmed the human breast, prompting to generous and noble deeds, to tender and touching expressions, to costly and precious sacrifices; and place it side by side with the divine love that chose you, the love that ransomed you, the love that called you, the love that soothes you, the love whose eyelid never closes, whose accents never change, whose warmth never chills, whose hand is never withdrawn– "the love of Christ which passes knowledge" and it is the very antithesis of selfishness. The love of Christ stands out in the 'history of the love', as the divinest, the holiest, the strongest of all love– unequaled, unparalleled, unsurpassed. Oh! there is no love like Christ's love! Trace its features.

1. The love of Christ is a REVEALING love. It uplifts the veil from the heart of God, and shows how that heart loves me. I would have known nothing of the love of my Father in heaven, but for the love of my Savior on earth. And that penitent, believing soul that feels the softest, gentlest pulse of Christ's love throbbing in his breast, knows more of the heart of God, sees more of the glory of God, and understands more of the character of God, than were earth and sky and sea to collect all their wonders and lay them at his feet.

2. The love of Christ is a CONDESCENDING love. No other love ever stooped like Christ's love. Go to Bethlehem and behold its lowliness, and as you return, pause awhile at Gethsemane, and gaze upon its sorrow, then pursue your way to Calvary, and learn, in the ignominy, in the curse, in the gloom, in the desertion, in the tortures, in the crimson tide of that cross– how low Christ's love has stooped. And still it stoops! It bends to all your circumstances. You can be conscious of the becloudings of no guilt it will not cancel, of the pressure of no sin it will not lighten, of the chafings of no cross it will not heal, of the depths of no sorrow it will not reach, of the dreary loneliness of no path it will not illumine and cheer. Oh! is there a home on earth where the love of Christ most loves to dwell, where you will oftener find, yes, always meet it? It is the heart-broken, contrite, and humbled for sin!

3. The love of Christ is a SELF-SACRIFICING love. "Christ has loved us, and has given himself for us, an offering and a sacrifice to God for a sweet-smelling savor." What a laborious life, what a suffering death was his, and all was but the out-paying, outpouring of his love. Every precept of the broken law he obeyed, every penalty of an exacting justice he endured. The path that conducted him from Bethlehem to Calvary wound its lonesome way through scenes of humiliation and insult, of trial and privation, the storm growing darker and darker, the thunder waxing louder and louder, and the lightning gleaming brighter and brighter, until its pivotal horrors gathered round the cross and crushed the Son of God! O marvelous love of Christ! what more could you do than you have done? To what lower depth of ignominy could you stoop? What darker sorrow could you endure? Where did another cross ever impale such a victim, or illustrate such love?

4. Nor is there any love so FORGIVING as Christ's love. Forgiveness of injury is an essential element of true affection. We cannot see how love can exist at the same moment and in the same breast with an unbending, unrelenting, unforgiving spirit. Real love is so unique and lofty a passion, so Godlike and divine in its nature and properties, we can not conceive of it but in alliance with every ennobling, elevating, and worthy sentiment. Selfishness, malignity, revenge, uncharitableness, and all evil speaking, are passions of our fallen and depraved humanity, so hateful and degrading, it would seem impossible that they should exist for an instant in the same atmosphere with true affection.

But a yet loftier form, a more sublime embodiment of love is presented to us in the love of God which is in Christ Jesus. God cannot love– we speak reverently– and not forgive. Those whom God loves, God pardons. That God regards every individual of the fallen race with a feeling of benevolence, is unquestionable; "for he makes his sun to rise on the evil and on the good, and sends rain on the just and on the unjust;" but those to whom the love of God extends his everlasting, his special, and his redeeming love– the gracious, the full, the eternal forgiveness of all sin likewise extends. God could not love a being and give that being over into the hands of a stern, avenging justice. Divine love will never lose the lowest and unworthiest object of its affections.

If, my reader, you feel conscious that you love God, though your affection be but as a smoldering ember, as a glimmering spark, be sure of this, that God first loved you; and loving, he has pardoned you; and pardoning, he will preserve you to his heavenly kingdom, that you may behold his glory, and enjoy his presence forever.

We repeat the remark, there is no love so forgiving as Christ's love. A human love may for an instant hesitate and falter; it may dwell upon the wrong inflicted, the injury done, the wound still bleeding; may, in its very muteness, speak in tones of inexpressible sadness, of confidence betrayed, of feelings lacerated, of friendship sported with, and the heart may find it difficult to take back the wrong-doer– the offender forgiven and the offense forgotten– to its embrace. But not so Jesus; he has canceled, obliterated, erased every shadow of a shade of his people's sins, and they shall come no more into remembrance. "Then Peter came to him, and said, Lord, how often shall my brother sin against me, and I forgive him? until seven times? Jesus said unto him– I say not unto you until seven times; but until seventy times seven."

Contrast this love, my reader– the forgiving disciple, the forgiving Savior– and then exclaim– "Who is a God like you, who pardons iniquity, and passes by the transgression of the remnant of his heritage? He retains not his anger forever, because he delights in mercy."

There is no love, too, so gentle, so patient, so enduring, as Christ's love. Again and again you have questioned it, wounded it, forsaken it; again and again you have returned to it with tears, confession, and humiliation, and have found it as unchilled and unchanged as his nature. It has borne with your doubts, has been silent beneath your murmurings, has veiled your infirmities, and has planted itself a thousand times over between you and your unseen and implacable foe. It has never declined with your fickleness, nor frozen with your coldness, nor upbraided you for your backslidings, but all the day long, tracking your wandering, winding way, it has hovered around you with a presence that has encircled you within its divine, all-enshrouding, and invincible shield. Truly, there is no love like Christ's!

Nor is there any love that so chimes with human grief as his. Born in sorrow, schooled in adversity, baptized in suffering, acquainted with grief in its every shape, it is just the love for which our sorrows pant. There is but one heart in this vast universe that can meet your case, O child of affliction! it is the divine, yet human heart of Christ. All other love and sympathy, the most intense and feeling, touches but the surface of our grief. Its trembling hand often irritates the wound it seeks to heal; or, perhaps, from the very intensity of its sympathy, catches the contagion of our grief, and sinks at our side helpless, hopeless, and despairing. Then it is the love of Christ approaches, touches us, and we are healed; speaks to us, and all is peace. "O unexampled love! Love nowhere to be found, less than divine."

How much of sacred meaning is contained in the prayer breathed by Paul on behalf of the Thessalonian saints– "The Lord direct your hearts into the love of God." The image is expressive. You have often, doubtless, trodden in pensive thought the sands which belt some expanded ocean, when the tide has ebbed, and have marked the undulating surface of reef and shallow that has traced and disfigured it. You have revisited the spot when that tide has rolled back in its majesty and fullness, and lo! not a vestige of the former scene appeared; every shallow is filled, every line of blemish is erased, and the blue waves toss their jocund heads as gracefully and musically as ever.

Such is the love of Christ! When this divine ocean recedes from your soul, you are filled with dismay at the spectacle that appears is one of emptiness, barrenness, and deformity. The love of Christ in the soul depressed, all is depressed. That ebbing tide has borne upon its receding wave the heart's last throb of gladness, and the soul's last gleam of hope, and nothing meets the eye but spiritual aridness and sin. Alarmed at the sad picture, you are roused to prayer, and you cry– "Restore unto me the joys of your salvation!" Your petition is accepted, and the response is heard, "I am returned to Jerusalem with mercies," and once more Christ's love flows back in gentle wavelets upon your soul, veiling every infirmity, and nothing but the sweetest melody breathes from your heaving bosom.

IV. No SAVIOR like Him.

There is no Savior like Christ. Sin is inventive; itself the greatest invention of all. It is Satan's infernal machine for destroying precious souls by the million! In nothing is his ingenuity and power more put forth than in constructing expedients of salvation other than the atoning sacrifice of the Lord Jesus Christ. But Jesus is the one and only Savior of men; "neither is there salvation in any other; for there is no other name under heaven given among men whereby we must be saved." It is the glory of Christ's salvation that it is perfectly adapted to every condition of our fallen and helpless humanity. Christianity is the only religion that fully recognizes the natural and utter depravity of our nature, and our consequent impotence to save ourselves. Jesus, therefore, is the Savior of sinners. He has undertaken to save us just as we are. He finds us a ruin, and recreates us; he finds us fallen, and raises us up; he finds us guilty, and he cleanses us; he finds us condemned, and he justifies us– all our salvation is in him. All the merit God requires, all the help man needs, all the grace and strength our salvation demands, dwells in infinite fullness in Christ.

My reader, your everlasting future of happiness or of woe depends upon your acceptance of Christ as your Savior! Compared with this, your vital union with the Lord Jesus– churches are nothing, sacraments are nothing, religious duties are nothing, rites and ceremonies are nothing– because Christ must be all in the momentous matter of your everlasting well-being. Nothing saves you but faith in Christ, and, possessing that faith, nothing shall condemn you. You may adopt the soundest creed, may join the most apostolic communion, and may observe the most rigid austerities, and yet not be a Christian. United by faith to Christ, you may be saved in any Church; separated from Christ, you can be saved in no Church; "for other foundation can no man lay than what is laid, which is Jesus Christ." What a Savior, then, is Christ!

That there should be to us lost sinners any Savior, is marvelous; but that there should be provided for us such a Savior as Christ is, so divine and human, so atoning and gracious, so able and willing, distances all thought, and is above all praise. None will he reject, who come to him. Oh! it is impossible to exaggerate this statement. All thought droops, all words fail in their attempt to show what a Savior Christ is to poor lost sinners. He saves to the uttermost. He saves from the lowest depth of ruin, from the loftiest height of guilt, from the farthest limit of sin, from the utmost verge of the yawning precipice, from the very mouth of hell! "Where sin has abounded, grace does much more abound."

If, abjuring all human merit, bewailing and deploring all sin, you accept as a free-grace bestowment, the salvation Christ wrought in his soul's travail on the cross, you shall be saved. If you stay away from Christ, your best righteousness will not preserve you from the eternal pains of hell. If you humbly and believingly come to Christ, your worst sins will not exclude you from the everlasting joys and blessedness of heaven. But it is of the utmost moment that you clearly recognize the only character and the sole ground on which Christ will save you. He will only save you "as a sinner", and on the ground of his finished work, his infinite merit, atoning blood, and righteousness. You must stand where the tax-collector stood; must kneel where the "woman who was a sinner" knelt; must feel with Saul of Tarsus, that you are the "chief of sinners," must look and appeal to him with the true penitence and simple faith of the dying malefactor, and you shall be saved!

Cling Closer to Him! Believer in Jesus! cling closer and closer to the Savior, for there is none like unto him! Let the life you live be a daily coming up out of self, into Christ. Place no limit to your transactions with Jesus. As yet you have but touched the edge of his ocean-fullness, you have but tasted that he is gracious, you have but crept beneath the hem of his ample robe. Oh! let this year be one of advance; your motto, "forward." The truth each day's history will but confirm you in is, "There is none like Christ." The more you trust to, and the more you draw from him, the deeper and sweeter will be your conviction and experience of this. It is a truth he intends you shall experimentally learn. He will have you prize, and love, and serve him above and beyond all others.

The process by which you reach this high and holy attainment may be trying, the path rugged and toilsome, the ascent steep and difficult; it may cost you many a severe pang, many a deep sigh, many a lonely tear, many a sad wrench; nevertheless, a clearer realization of this truth, "none like Christ, none so near, none so powerful, none so precious," will more than recompense for all. Christ, in the sufficiency of his love and grace, will come and fill the blank, and soothe the pain, and dry the tear, and you shall look up, and with more than a seraph's rapture exclaim– "Whom have I in heaven but you? and there is none upon earth that I desire beside you."

V. No TEACHER like Him.

There is no teacher like Christ. Upon this point we can venture but a single remark. The Anointed of God, it is his office to reveal to us the great things of the Gospel. We are truly and savingly taught only as we are taught by him. Thankful for human teachers, we yet must exclaim– "Who teaches like Christ?" With immediate access to our minds, and a quick avenue to our hearts, by one text, by one trial, and by one circumstance of our history, he can, in a moment, bring us into the experience of the deepest and most spiritual truth. Who teaches with the authority, or with the skill, or with the patience and gentleness of Christ? Become his student, beloved reader, enter as a disciple his school, and the Holy Spirit, whose office it is to glorify Christ, will lead you into all truth. Oh! that this may be a year of deeper, more spiritual teaching! Oh! that we may know more of our own nothingness and insufficiency, and more of Christ's fullness, loveliness, and love! Lord that which I know not, teach me, for who teaches to profit like yourself?

VI. No FRIEND like Him.

There is no Friend like Christ. Beloved, it is possible that having many friends, you need yet one. God has, perhaps, endowed you with a nature keenly susceptible, your heart expanding to the warm and genial influence of true friendship. There is in your breast the responsive power of love, yet yearning for its object. Or, perhaps, the cold blast of sorrow has swept over the garden of your confiding affections, and the finest feelings of your nature, torn from the support to which they clung, lie broken, wounded, and bleeding. You yearn for a friend, in the wisdom of whose counsel, in the depth of whose affection, in the delicacy of whose sympathy, in the patience of whose endurance you can implicitly and ever rely; and from whose presence nothing for a moment separates. That friend is Christ! "I call you not servants, but friends," is his gracious avowal of the relation. "He is a friend that sticks closer than a brother."

There is not a friend on earth who loves you with his affection, who compassionates you with his sympathy, or is so powerful, so faithful, so near to you as Christ. Human friends do, indeed, divide our cares and double our joys; but Jesus does more. He takes all our cares upon himself, absorbs all our sorrows in himself, and makes all his joy our own. Let this be a year of closer friendship with Christ! Confide in his love, avail yourself of his power, and abase yourself worthy of so precious a friend. Beware, in your dealings with him, of distrust, of shyness, of cooled affection. Place in him your unquestioning confidence, and give him your undivided heart. Let not the sad memories of past fickleness and failure fling their dark shadows on the future, but enter upon that future surrendering yourself afresh to Christ as your best Friend.

Oh! there is none like him. Leave him for a while, though you may, for others, you return to him again with a yet deeper conviction of his superiority, exclaiming– "I find no friend like Christ. No love soothes me, no smile gladdens me, no voice cheers me, no arm supports me as his!"

You are entering upon a year which must be one of human in-firmity, toil, and trial. Remember your chief, your best, your only Friend took upon him all your human infirmities, is identified with all your desires, and is acquainted with all your lonely sor-rows. Now that he is elevated to the loftiest reach of purity, to the highest degree of dignity and glory, and that that heart, once the abode of overshadowing grief, is all sunshine now, but fits him all the more exquisitely as the all-powerful, all-helpful, all-loving, all-tender, ever-present Friend and companion of your homeward path to God.

O Christ! you ever have been, you are, and you shall ever be my Friend! In adversity, I will hide beneath your sheltering wing; in sorrow, I will nestle within your loving bosom; in weakness, I will entwine around your upholding arm; in need, I will repair to your boundless resources; in sickness, in languor, and in suffering, I will enfold around me your all-divine, all-human, all-pervading, all-soothing sympathy–

"And when I die,
Receive me, I'll cry,
For, Lord, you have loved me,
I cannot tell why."

VII. No SERVICE like His.

And what service can be placed in competition with the service of Christ? The profession of Christian discipleship involves a service. The Christian life must needs have scope for the unfolding of its powers, and a field for the employment of its energies. But for the activity of Christianity our religion would become paralyzed and be dwarfed. It is a wise and merciful arrangement of its Author, that for the vital forces– the muscle and nerve and life of our Christian-ity– there should be provided a sphere ample and appropriate for their full development and play.

The graces implanted in the soul– graces instinct with all the energy and power of the divine, before whose invincible might the fiercest assaults of the foe have been repelled, and the armies of the aliens put to flight– would become shriveled and collapsed, a moral atrophy seizing the whole soul, but for the service which summons them to action. Christ's kingdom supplies the appropri-ate and commanding sphere. The field of your exertion may be ex-tended or circumscribed, just as God appoints. It may be the vast amphitheater encircled by a great crowd of witnesses, gazing intently and anxiously upon your wrestling with sin and your battle with error; or, it may be some shaded nook, secluded from every eye, unaided and uncheered by human sympathy. Perhaps the sacred enclosure of home, or the night-watches of a sick-room, or the self-denying task of instructing a crude and sluggish class in the simple elements of the Gospel– yet is it Christ's service which engages you, and as such, it is perfect freedom and exquisite delight.

And truly there is no service to be compared with it– so ennobling, so satisfying, so joy-inspiring– or that brings with it so much of present and rich reward. Servant of Christ! keep good heart! Listen to your Master's feet behind you, upholding and cheering you on. He will soon come and pay you your full wages– will wipe the sweat of toil from your brow, and wreathe it with an amaranthine crown of glory, honor, and immortality. Then comes the welcome and reward– "Well done, good and faithful servant, enter into the joy of your Lord."

With such a service, and such a recompense, who, with but a spark of the love of Christ in his heart, will not exclaim– "Here, Lord, am I, what will you have me to do?" I have but one life– you have bought it with your life-blood– may it be yours– yours wholly, forever yours."

Christian reader, be up and doing– why do you stand all the day idle? Go, work in your Lord's vineyard. With a significance more profound, and with an earnestness more intense than that with which the words were uttered by the Mohammedan chief, pointing his sword to earth and then up to heaven, would we say to you– "Here is the place of labor; there is the place of rest."

'Tis not for man to trifle; life is brief,
And sin is here;
Our age is but the falling of a leaf,
A dropping tear.
We have no time to sport away the hours;
All must be earnest in a world like ours.
Not many lives, but only one have we;
One, only one–
How sacred should that one life ever be–
That narrow span!
Day after day filled up with blessed toil,
Hour after hour still bringing in new spoil."

There is no friend like Christ! The truth upon which we have been endeavoring to concentrate your thoughts, and with which we would yet a few moments longer detain you, is one of great practical influence. It chimes with every event, circumstance, and situation of your life. Let your faith deal with it as a divine verity, as a practical reality, that in whatever position God places you, he intends, by his dealings in providence, and by his teaching in grace, to bring you into the deeper experience of this the most precious of all experimental and practical truths– "No one can meet my case like Christ."

Whatever, through this year, your position may be– and I will hypothetically place it– let faith reason thus– "I am in great adversity; why should I resort to the help of man, he may fail me– there is none like Christ. I am in profound grief, my heart is melted within me; why should I repair to the soothing of human sympathy, it may disappoint me– there is none like Christ. I am in a great strait; insurmountable difficulties, inextricable perplexities weave their network around my path, and I am at my wit's end; why should I betake myself to human counsel– it may mislead me– there is none like Christ. My future looks dark and lowering– disease undermining my health– my energies failing, and the duties, responsibilities, and labors for which I have taxed my utmost powers, all lie untouched and neglected, yet why should I despond– there is none like Christ. My temporal circumstances are narrowing, resources fail me, poverty, with its humiliating attendants, stares me in the face, yet why should I yield to unbelief– there is none lice Christ. My corruptions are strong, my temptations irresistible, my sins many, my doubts and fears weigh me down to the dust, yet why should I despair– there is none like Christ. I am approaching the solemn hour of death, heart and flesh are failing me, and the veil of eternity is slowly rising to my view, yet why should I fear, and tremble, and shrink back, I have committed my soul to my Savior, and– there is none like Christ."

And, oh! what a mercy that you have never found one that could for a moment take his place; that, separated, perhaps exiled from all others, you are enclosed to Christ alone, nor wish another being to share your confidence or divide your affection with him. It is possible that you have made the experiment. You have traveled the circle of creation's good, have sipped at many springs, have gathered many flowers, have sought repose in many an embowered spot, but all have failed. You have returned to your true rest, exclaiming– "None like Christ. I find no love so soothing as his, no friendship so true, so gentle as his, no communion like communion with him. Christ is my all and in all."

Does the **world** challenge– "What is your beloved more than another beloved?" Your answer is at hand– "My beloved bore my sins, opened in his heart a fountain in which I am washed whiter than snow. My beloved sustains my burdens, counsels my perplexities, heals my wounds, dries my tears, supplies my needs, bears with my infirmities, upholds my steps, and cheers my pathway to the tomb. My beloved will be with me in the valley of the shadow of death, and with his presence I shall fear no evil. My beloved has gone to prepare a place for me in the many-mansioned house of my Father, and will come again and receive me to himself, that where he is, I may be also. My beloved will walk with me in the gold-paved streets of the new Jerusalem, will lead me to fountains of living waters, and will wipe every tear from my eyes. This is my beloved, and this is my Friend!"

Therefore Stand Firm. And yet have we need of constant vigilance, lest we should not always and in everything give Christ the preeminence. The rival interests, and the antagonistic forces of the world and the flesh are in perpetual play. These demand that, with the prophet, we should "stand continually upon the watchtower in the daytime, and be set in our wards whole nights." Should you discover any encroachment of your worldly calling upon the claims Christ has to your time and service, any rival affections to the claims he has to your whole heart, any secret demur to the claims he has to your unreserved obedience; should you, in a word, detect the undue ascendency or influence of any one being or object whose presence and power tends to shade the beauty, lessen the attractions, weaken the supremacy, or share the throne of Christ in your soul– that being and that object must be relinquished at once and forever!

Oh! what competitor can stand side by side with Christ? No minister, or pastor, or church, or friend, or companion, can bear a moment's comparison with Jesus. Not one who can assist you, defend you, provide for you, or bear with you as Jesus, who when the snow-flakes of wintry adversity fall thick and fast, and its cold blast moans drearily around you, will not leave yet side, who will be first to enter the house of woe, across whose threshold the loved remains have just been borne, to speak words of comfort to your bereaved heart; who will sustain you in languor, bend over you in sickness, and when the last look, before the eye is fixed and glazed, and the last breath, before the lips are mute and immovable in death, shall come, will be with you, viewless and noiseless to the attendant watchers, sustaining your spirit in the parting hour, then bearing it in his own warm bosom to the home eternally made ready. Then cling and adhere to Christ, and in all things give him the preeminence.

"Enthrone the precious Savior in your heart,
Let all your homage unto him be paid;
Allow no idol to usurp in part
The glory due to him who all things made.
In thought, word, deed, your life to him be given,
You shall be blessed on earth, and saved in heaven."

Be Faithful to His Word. There is yet another caution I would venture to give in reference to some of the social and popular movements of the day, the tendency of which, without due vigilance on the part of the sincere and earnest friends of true religion, may be adverse to its best interests, fatally injurious to the individuals contemplated by these movements, and subversive of the supremacy of Christ and his truth. We hail with gratitude and hope all efforts to advance "social science" and intellectual improvement, provided those endeavors are sustained and sanctified by Christian principle. I am thoroughly convinced that true national advancement can only be successfully secured by the power of a living Christianity. All other modes of elevating the masses utterly fail of reaching them. It is impossible to close the eye to the fact that, after all the exertions of our literary and scientific institutions, our libraries, reading-rooms, and lectures, there teems outside and far beyond our efforts, a vast outlying population of living beings, dwelling in ignorance and neglect, each one of whom might give utterance to the exclamation– "No man has cared for my soul!"

By what agency are we to compass and by what means are we to instruct them? We at once answer, by the feet of the city and the rural missionary, and by the sole instrument of Christ's Gospel. But widely different from this is the object promoted by "social science" and its kindred associations. And what is the result? We are advancing in secular knowledge and science, but, at the same time, we are equally advancing in worldliness, luxury, and indulgence; in extravagance of dress, and modes of life that, in numerous cases, far overtop reasonable and legitimate income. The consequences must be serious! The history of nations is luminous in the testimony it bears to the fact that high perfection in art and science, in intellectual improvement, luxury, and indulgence, apart from the conservative influence of Christianity, has ever been the culminating point that has marked their decadence and dissolution. We have passed through one phase of our national history, and "hero-worship" is nearly giving place to the worship of "social science," secular knowledge, and intellectual advancement. I cannot look but with the most painful apprehension and alarm upon the unchristianized condition toward which we are as a nation fast drifting. Compromise at home, and neutrality abroad, is gradually blotting Christianity from our national escutcheon. It seriously behooves the ministers of the Gospel, our devout statesmen and senators, to be fully awake. If we are to retain the position God has given us in the scale of nations, or to rise to a yet loftier altitude of moral greatness and power, it will not be by the means of social science, worldly knowledge, wealth, luxury, and refinement– but by the influence of a living, vitalizing Christianity alone!

The Bible and its religion must be paramount; Christ and his Gospel must have the preeminence. Reason and learning must stand at the bar of Revelation, reverence its precepts, adopt its principles, and obey its voice. The moment that finds this nation glorying in her strength, in her wisdom, in her wealth, in her prowess, in her social progress, and in her high civilization, will date the beginning of her decline, and foreshadow the certainty of her downfall as a great, religious people; and her last history, like that of Greece and Rome, will be written in mourning, lamentation, and woe. Let the apostles and promoters of social science and of secular knowledge solemnly beware how, in the advancement of their objects, they ignore our Bible and abjure our God!

Be Spiritually Minded. It is an important practical deduction from the subject of these pages, that if true godliness is anything to us, it surely must be everything. There is no principle God has more closely and universally calculated in the universe than 'harmony'. And it is this nice adjustment, this perfect balance, and exquisite symmetry, everywhere pervading his works, which proves the mind that planned and the power that executed to be one and the same– divine.

Now it is this same harmony, as exhibited in true godliness, which illustrates its beauty and augments its power. How much is true religion shorn of its strength by the lack of more spiritual-mindedness in its professors! The worldly amusements to which many addict themselves– the opera, the card-playing, the ball, the gay party, the novel-reading, the luxurious living, the extravagant customs in which multitudes of religious professors, church members and communicants indulge, are **sad blots** upon their avowed Christianity, and effectual hindrances to the advancement of religion in their own souls and in the world. Oh! that with us vital religion– the pure, simple, self-denying, unearthly religion of Christ– might be paramount; its holy influence permeating our whole being, and giving form and tint and direction to all our engagements and conduct.

Difficulties we shall, indeed, have to overcome in the world, and, perhaps, opposing influences in our own homes; nevertheless, if Christ sees that our hearts are set upon ruling our lives by his divine precept, "Seek first the kingdom of God and his righteousness," he will aid our holy strivings and give his grace that, in our principles, our spirit, and our conduct, yes, in all things and everywhere, Christ may have the preeminence.

My reader, what is **your** "beloved"? If it is not Christ, what is it? The world? the creature? wealth? self? Are these the objects you place in competition with the Redeemer, and prefer to a religious life, a happy death, and a glorious eternity? Oh! what will they avail you when Christ, the Savior you have slighted, despised, and neglected, cites you to his judgment bar? Without the experience of a real conversion, of the new birth, of a saving interest in Jesus, should you die this year, you are forever lost! Pause, solemnly pause, upon the threshold of a new period of your probation, and ask the Holy Spirit to enthrone the Savior upon your loving, believing heart, that henceforth Christ may be the first, Christ the chief, Christ preeminent; so that for you to live or die may truly and emphatically be CHRIST; and then Christ and you will be together through eternity!

There is None like Him. Such is the truth, child of God, your heavenly Father has given you to learn through this coming year– None like Christ! Could he bring you into the experience of a truth more needful, more sanctifying, or more precious? Impossible! Strive after a closer walk, a more childlike transfer of every care, anxiety, and need to your heavenly Father, and his beloved Son, your elder brother. "He cares for you." Do not overlook today, in your anxious thoughts about the morrow. Travel not out of the present into the future. The grace that supports, the love that comforts, the resources that supply today's need, will, with tomorrow's demand, be ready at your hand. Do justice to the solemn present, and live with the same calm reliance upon God, and looking to Jesus, as if there but one second of time intervening between you and your heavenly home. Make the prayer your own of one of the earliest missionaries of the Cross to Ireland– "May the strength of God pilot me this day, the power of God preserve me, the wisdom of God instruct me, the eye of God view me, the ear of God hear me, the hand of God protect me, the way of God direct me, the shield of God defend me. Christ be with me, Christ before me, Christ after me, Christ in me, Christ under me, Christ over me, Christ at my right, Christ at my left, Christ at this side, Christ at that side, Christ in the heart of each person whom I speak to, Christ in the mouth of each person who speaks to me, Christ in each eye which sees me, Christ in each ear which hears me. Salvation is the Lord's, salvation is Christ's. May your salvation, O Lord! be always with us." (Patrick's prayer on his going to preach before the King of Ireland)

Imitating the spirit, and adopting the petitions of this remarkable prayer, your daily, happy, and holy experience and testimony will be– "None but Christ, none like Christ."

"I'll not leave Jesus– never, never!
Ah! what can more precious be?
Rest, and joy, and light are ever
In his hand to give to me.
All things that can satisfy,
Having Jesus, these have I."

Love has bound me fast to him,
I am his, and he is mine;
Daily I for pardon ask him,
Answers he with peace divine.
On that rock my trust is laid,
And I rest beneath its shade.

Without Jesus, earth would weary,
Seem almost like hell to me;
But if Jesus I have near me,
Earth is almost heaven to me.
Am I hungry? He does give
Bread on which my soul does live.

Oh! how light upon my shoulder
Lies my cross, now grown so small.
For the Lord is my upholder,
Fits it to me, softens all.
Neither shall it always stay–
Patience! it will pass away!"

CHRIST'S SYMPATHY TO WEARY PILGRIMS

What a boundless, fathomless ocean!

Eternal love moved the heart of Jesus to relinquish . . .
  heaven for earth;
  a diadem for a cross;
  the robe of divine majesty for the garment of our nature;
by taking upon Himself the leprosy of our sin.
Oh, the infinite love of Christ!

What a boundless, fathomless ocean!

Ask the ransomed of the Lord, whose *chains* He has dissolved, whose *dungeon* He has opened, whose *liberty* He has conferred — if there ever was love like His!

What shall we say of *the ransom price*? It was the richest, the costliest, that Heaven could give! He gave *Himself* for us! What more could He do? He gave Himself; body, soul and spirit. He gave His time, His labor, His blood, His life, His ALL — as the price for our ransom, the cost of our redemption. He carried the wood and reared the altar. Then, bearing His bosom to the stroke of the uplifted and descending arm of the Father — He paid the price of our salvation in the warm lifeblood of His heart!

What a boundless, fathomless ocean! How is it that we feel the force and exemplify the practical influence of this amazing, all commanding truth so faintly? Oh, the desperate depravity of our nature! Oh, the deep iniquity of our iniquitous hearts! Will not the blood-drops of Jesus move us? Will not the agonies of the cross influence us? Will not His dying love constrain us to a more heavenly life?

Lean hard!

"Cast your burden upon the Lord — and He shall sustain you." Psalm 55:22

It is by an act of simple, prayerful faith that we transfer our cares and anxieties, our sorrows and needs, to the Lord. Jesus invites you come and lean upon Him, and to lean with all your might upon that *arm* that balances the universe, and upon that *bosom* that bled for you upon the soldier's spear!

But you doubtingly ask, "Is the Lord able to do this thing for me?" And thus, while you are debating a matter about which there is not the shadow of a shade of doubt, the burden is crushing your gentle spirit to the dust. And all the while Jesus stands at your side and lovingly says, "Cast your burden upon Me — and I will sustain you. I am God Almighty! I bore the load of your sin and condemnation up the steep of Calvary; and the same power of omnipotence, and the same strength of love that bore it all for you then — is prepared to bear your need and sorrow now. Roll it all upon Me! Child of My love! **Lean hard!** Let Me feel the pressure of your care. I know your burden, child! I shaped it — I poised it in My own hand and made no proportion of its weight to your unaided strength. For even as I laid it on, I said I shall be near, and while she leans on Me, this burden shall be Mine, not hers. So shall I keep My child within the encircling arms of My own love. Here lay it down! Do not fear to impose it on a shoulder which upholds the government of worlds! Yet closer come! You are not near enough! I would embrace your burden, so I might feel My child reposing on My bosom. You love Me! I know it. Doubt not, then. But, loving me, **lean hard!**"

The flaming sword of justice quenched in the holy, loving bosom of Jesus!

"He Himself bore our sins in His body on the tree!" 1 Peter 2:24

The most significant and appalling demonstration of God's holiness that the universe ever beheld, infinitely distancing and transcending every other — is the sufferings and death of His only and beloved Son! The cross of Calvary exhibits God's hatred and punishment of sin in a way and to an extent which the annihilation of millions of worlds, swept from the face of the universe by the broom of His wrath, could never have done!

Behold the most solemn display of God's hatred of sin! Finding the sins of the Church upon Christ as its Surety, Substitute, and Savior — *the wrath of God was poured out upon Him without measure!* Finding the sins of His people laid upon His Son — God emptied upon His holy soul, all the vials of His wrath due to their transgressions! Go, my soul, to Calvary, and learn how *holy God* is, and what a monstrous thing *sin* is, and how imperiously, solemnly, and holily bound, Jehovah is to punish it, either in the person of the sinner, or in the person of a Surety. Never was the Son of God dearer to the Father than at the very moment that *the sword of divine justice, flaming and flashing, pierced to its hilt His holy heart!*

But it was the wrath of God, not against His beloved Son — but against the sins which met on Him when presenting Himself on the cross as the substitutionary sacrifice and offering for His

Church. He gave Himself *for us!*

What a new conception must angels have formed of the exceeding sinfulness of sin, when they beheld **the flaming sword of justice quenched in the holy, loving bosom of Jesus!** And in what a dazzling light does this fact place the marvelous love of God to sinners! Man's sin — and God's love; the indescribable enormity of the one — and the immeasurable greatness of the other; are exhibited in the *cross of Christ* as nowhere else.

Oh, to learn experimentally these two great facts: sin's infinite hatefulness — and love's infinite holiness! The love of God in giving His Son to die; the love of Christ in dying; the essential turpitude and unmitigated enormity of sin, which demanded a *Sacrifice* so Divine, so holy, and so precious!

Plunge into this fathomless, boundless ocean of love!

Christ is wonderful in His love. Love was the first and eternal *link* in the *golden chain* lowered from the highest throne in heaven — down to the lowest depth of earth. That Christ should love *us* was the beginning of wonders. When we endeavor to comprehend that love, measure it, fathom it, scale it — we learn that it has heights we cannot reach, depths we cannot sound, lengths and breadths we cannot measure! Such love, such *divine* love, such *infinite* love, such *everlasting* love, such *redeeming*, such *dying* love — is an ocean whose eternal waves waft into our fallen world, every wonder of God and of heaven.

That Jesus should love such beings as *us* — that He should love us while we were yet sinners — that He should set His heart upon us, choose us, die for us, save us, and finally bring us to glory, knowing what we were, and what we would prove to be — oh, *this is wondrous love indeed!*

Plunge into this fathomless, boundless ocean of love, O sin-burdened one! It will cover all your sins, it will efface all your guilt; it will flood over all your unworthiness — and, floating upon its golden waves, it will gently waft you to the shore of eternal blessedness!

How often have you wondered *why* Christ should set His heart upon such a one as you! And is it not a wonder that, amid all your fickleness and backslidings, and cold, base returns — this love of God towards you has not chilled or changed? But do not rest, do not be satisfied with your present limited experience of Christ's wonderful love. It is so marvelously great. This *ocean of love* is **so fathomless, boundless, and inexhaustible** — that you may plunge, with all your infirmities, sins, and sorrows, into its fullness, exclaiming, *"O, the depth!"* The well is deep! Drink abundantly, O beloved!

"May you have the power to understand, as all God's people should — how wide, how long, how high, and how deep His love is. May you experience the love of Christ, though it is too great to understand fully!" Ephesians 3:18-19

Love suffering, and bleeding, and expiring!

The love of Christ! Such a precious theme! Of it, can we ever weary? Never! Its greatness, can we ever know? Never! Its plenitude, can we fully contain? Never! Its depths cannot be fathomed, its dimensions cannot be measured! It passes knowledge! All that Jesus did for His people was but the unfolding and expression of His love.

Traveling to Bethlehem — I see *love incarnate!*

Tracking His steps as He went about doing good — I see *love laboring!*

Visiting the house of Bethany — I see *love sympathizing!*

Standing by the grave of Lazarus — I see *love weeping!*

Entering the gloomy precincts of Gethsemane — I see *love sorrowing!*

Passing on to Calvary — I see **love suffering, and bleeding, and expiring!**

The whole scene of His life — is but an unfolding of the deep, and awesome, and precious mystery of redeeming love!

"May you have the power to understand, as all God's people should — how wide, how long, how high, and how deep His love is. May you experience the love of Christ, though it is too great to understand fully!" Ephesians 3:18-19

It is I!

"Take courage! It is I! Do not be afraid." Mark 6:50

Listen, then, to the *voice of Jesus in the storm!*

It is I who raised the *tempest* in your soul — and will control it.

It is I who sent your *affliction* — and will be with you in it.

It is I who kindled the *furnace* — and will watch the flames, and bring you through it.

It is I who formed your *burden,* who carved your *cross* — and who will strengthen you to bear it.

It is I who mixed your *cup of grief* — and will enable you to drink it with meek submission to your Father's will.

It is I who took from you *worldly substance,* who *bereft* you of your child, of the wife of your bosom, of the husband of your youth — and will be infinitely better to you than husband, wife, or child.

It is I who has done it ALL!

I make the clouds My chariot, and clothe Myself with the tempest as with a garment. The *night* hour is My time of coming, and the dark, surging waves are the pavement upon which I walk. Take courage! *It is I!* Do not be afraid.

It is I — your Friend, your Brother, your Savior! I am causing all the circumstances of your life to work together for your good.

It is I who permitted . . .

the *enemy* to assail you,

the *slander* to blast you,

the *unkindness* to wound you,

the *need* to press you!

Your affliction did not spring out of the ground, but came down from above — a heaven-sent blessing disguised as an angel of light, clad in a robe of ebony.

I have sent all in love!

This *sickness* is not unto death — but for the glory of God.

This *bereavement* shall not always bow you to the earth, nor drape in changeless gloom your life. *It is I* who ordered, arranged, and controlled it all!

In every stormy wind,

in every darksome night,

in every lonesome hour,

in every rising fear,

— the voice of Jesus shall be heard,

saying, *"Take courage! It is I! Do not be afraid."*

The personal attractions of Jesus

Yes, He is altogether lovely! This is my Beloved, and this is my Friend!" Song of Songs 5:16

The personal attractions of Jesus are all inviting and irresistible!

His *love* wins us.
His *glory* charms us.
His *beauty* attracts us.
His *sympathy* soothes us.
His *gentleness* subdues us.
His *faithfulness* inspires us.

He is the "altogether lovely One!"

Jesus is all that is tender in love.
Jesus is all that is wise in counsel.
Jesus is all that is patient and kind.
Jesus is all that is faithful in friendship.
Jesus is all that is balmy, soothing, and healing.
The heart of Jesus is ever loving towards His children.
The disposition of Jesus is ever kind towards His children.
The nature of Jesus is ever sympathizing towards His children.
Jesus is your Brother, your Friend, your Redeemer.
As your Brother — He knows the need of His brethren in adversity.
As your Friend — He shows Himself friendly.
As your Redeemer — He has redeemed your soul from sin and hell.
Jesus has ascended up on high to take possession of heaven on your behalf, and to prepare a place for you!
Upon His heart He wears your name as a precious pearl in the priestly breastplate.
There is . . .
not a moment of your time,
nor an event of your life,
nor a circumstance of your daily history,
nor a mental or spiritual emotion of yours —
in which you are not borne upon the love, and
remembered in the ceaseless intercession of Christ.
Yes, He is altogether lovely! This is my Beloved, and this is my Friend!" Song of Songs 5:16
Can you stand before this love — this love so precious, so great, so enduring, so self-consuming, so changeless; and know that . . .
for you was this offering,
for you this cross,
for you this agony,
for you this scorn and insult,
for you this death —

and feel no sensibility, no emotion, no love to Jesus? Impossible!

Do not be cast down, then, in vain regrets that your love to Christ is so frigid, so fickle, so dubious. Go and muse upon the reality and the greatness of the Savior's love to you — and if love can inspire love, while you muse, the fire will burn, and your soul shall be all in flame with love to Jesus!

He will be our guide even unto death!

"For this God is our God forever and ever! **He will be our guide even unto death!**" Psalm 48:14

The world passes away. Everything here in this present world is changing.

"Life is like a painted dream;
 Like the rapid summer stream;
 Like the fleeting meteor's ray;
 Like the shortest winter's day;
 Like the fitful breeze that sighs;
 Like the waning flame that dies;
 Darting, dazzling on the eye;
Fading in eternity!"
 A rope of sand,
 a spider's web,
 a silken thread,
 a passing shadow,
 an ebbing wave,
are the most fitting and expressive emblems of all things belonging to this present earthly state.

The *homes* that sheltered us in childhood — we leave.

The *land* which gave us birth — we leave.

The *loved ones* who encircled our hearths — pass away.

The *friends* of early years — depart.

And the world that was so sunny, and life that was so sweet — is all beclouded and embittered — the whole scenery of existence changed into wintry gloom. *Such are the saddening, depressing effects of life's vicissitudes.*

But in the midst of all, "This God is our God forever and ever!" All *beings* change — but God. All *things* change — but heaven. The evolutions of *time* revolve, the *events* of earth go onward, but He upon whom all things hang, and by whom all events are shaped and controlled, moves not. "For I am the Lord, I change not."

Our *affairs* may alter.

Our *circumstances* may change.

Our *relations* and *friends* may depart one by one.

Our *souls* in a single day pass through many fluctuations of spiritual feeling.

But He who chose us to be His own, and who has kept us to the present moment — is our covenant God and Father forever and ever, and will never throw us off and cast us away.

"For this God is our God forever and ever! He will be our guide even unto death!"

For me a worm!

"The Lord Jesus Christ, who gave Himself for our sins" Galatians 1:3-4

"He is the atoning sacrifice for our sins" 1 John 2:2

O what an astonishing truth is this! The Son of God offering Himself up a sacrifice for sin! He who knew no sin — who was holy, harmless, and undefiled — not one thought of evil in His heart — yet made sin, or a sin offering! O the magnitude of the thought! If God Himself had not declared it, we could not have believed it, though an angel's trumpet had announced it.

O blessed and adorable Immanuel! Was this the *end* and *design* of Your intense and mysterious sufferings? Was it that You should obey, bear the sin, endure the curse, and bow Your head in death — that I might go free? Was it in my stead, and in my behalf?

O unexampled love! O infinite and free grace! That God should become incarnate — that the Holy One should so take upon Him sin, as to be dealt with by stern justice as though He were Himself the sinner — that He should drain the cup of wrath, give His back to the smiters, endure the shame and the spitting, and at last be suspended upon the cross, and pour out His last drop of most precious blood — *and all this for me! For me a rebel!* **For me a worm!** *For me the chief of sinners!* "The Son of God, who loved me and gave Himself for me!" Galatians 2:20. Be astonished, O heavens! and be amazed, O earth! Was ever love like this?

The tears of Jesus!

"Jesus wept." John 11:35

These are among the most wonderful words recorded in the Bible. They mark the most exquisitely tender, touching, and expressive incident in His whole life. "Jesus wept" — wept from emotion, wept from sympathy. Is there a more consolatory, soothing view of

Christ's love than this? *It is a compassionate, sympathizing, weeping love!*

The *sympathy* of Jesus never wearies or slumbers, it never chills or forgets.

It entwines with our every cross.

It attaches to our every burden.

It frosts with sparkling light, each darkling cloud.

It is not the vapid sentiment of fiction, nor the morbid sympathy of romance. It is a divine-human reality. *It is the sympathetic love of the Incarnate God!*

Let your faith, then, repose with confidence on the reality of Christ's sympathy with your grief. Oh how sacred and precious are the tears of divine love — **the tears of Jesus!** Soothed and sustained by such a sympathy as Christ's, we may well drink meekly the *bitter cup* which our Father mingles. We can well afford to be severed from all other sympathy, and weep out our sorrow in lonely places — with Jesus sympathizing with us . . .

by the couch of languor,

by the bed of darkness, and

at the grave of buried love.

O afflicted one, tempest-tossed and not comforted, do not refuse this *cup of consolation* which the Holy Spirit, the Comforter, would give you — the sympathy of your Lord and Savior, your Friend and Brother in the time of your calamity. Yield yourself to its irresistible power, and it will draw you submissively to His feet, and hush to rest your sobbing heart upon His bosom!

Why, then, these fears? Why this distrust?

Jesus has all the treasures of the everlasting covenant, all the fullness of the Godhead, all the resources of the universe — in His keeping, and at His disposal!

Look at the *starry sky* — Jesus strewed it with its jewelry.

Look at that *enchanting landscape* — Jesus enameled it with its loveliness.

Look at that *cloud-capped mountain* — Jesus reared it.

Look at that *beauteous lily* — Jesus painted it.

Look at that *soaring bird* — Jesus feeds it.

He, with whom is all this strength and beauty — is your Brother! Are you not better and dearer to Him than these? He has loved and chosen you from all eternity, ransomed you with His blood, and inhabited you by His Spirit. **Why, then, these fears? Why this**

distrust? All He requires of you is to bring . . .

your *emptiness* — to His fullness;

your *grief* — to His sympathy;

your *confusion* — to His unerring wisdom;

your *temptations and trials* — to His sheltering wing.

Spread your case before Him in the humble confidence of a child. Listen to His words, "I give them eternal life, and they will never perish — ever! No one will snatch them out of My hand!" John 10:28

Christ's sleepless vigilance over His people!

"Surely I am with you always, to the very end of the age!" Matthew 28:20

What an exalted and endearing truth is **Christ's sleepless vigilance over His people!** Imagine yourself threading your way along a most difficult and perilous path, every step of which is attended with pain and hazard, and is taken with hesitancy and doubt. Unknown to you and unseen — there is One hovering around you each moment . . .

checking each false step,

guiding each doubtful one,

soothing each sorrow,

and supplying each need. All is calm and silent. Not a sound is heard, not a movement is seen; and yet, to your amazement, just at the critical moment, the needed support comes — you know not from where, you know not from whom! This is no picture of imagination — but a divine reality.

Are you a child of God on your *pilgrimage to paradise* by an intricate and a perilous way? Jesus is near to you at each moment, unseen and often unknown. You have at times stood speechless with awe at the strange interposition on your behalf, of *providence* and of *grace* — when no visible sign indicated the source of your help. There was no echo of footfall at your side, no flitting of shadow athwart your path. No law of nature was altered nor suspended, the sun did not stand still, nor did the heavens open. And yet deliverance, strange and effectual deliverance, came at a moment most unexpected, yet most needed.

It was Jesus your *Redeemer*, your *Brother*, your *Shepherd*, and your *Guide!* He it was who, hovering around you — unknown and unobserved, kept you as the apple of His eye, and sheltered you in the hollow of His hand. It was He who armed you with bravery for the fight — who poured strength into your spirit — and grace into your heart, when the full weight of calamity pressed upon them. Thus has He always been to His children.

The eye that neither slumbers nor sleeps — was upon you! He knew in what *furnace* you were placed, and was there to *temper* the flame when it seemed the severest. He saw your frail vessel struggling through the *tempest* — and He came to your rescue at the height of the storm!

How has He proved this in seasons of difficulty and doubt! How often, at a crisis the most critical of your history, the Lord has appeared for you! Your *lack* has been supplied — your *doubt* has been solved — and your *perplexity* has been guided. He has delivered your *soul* from death — your *eyes* from tears — and your *feet* from falling. You are never for an instant out of His *heart* — out of His *thoughts* — out of His *hands* — or out of His *eye!*

Go then, and lay your weariness on Christ!

Take your bereaved, stricken and bleeding heart to Him!

What is your sorrow?

Has the hand of death smitten?

Is the beloved one removed?

Has the desire of your eyes been taken away with a stroke?

But who has done it?

Jesus has done it! Death was only His *messenger*. Your Jesus has done it. The Lord has taken away. And what has He removed? Your wife? Ah, Jesus has all the tenderness that your wife ever had. Her love was only a *drop* from the *ocean* of love which is in His heart. Is it your husband? Jesus is better to you than ten husbands. Is it your parent, your child, your friend, your all of earthly bliss? Is the *cistern* broken? Is the *earthen vessel* dashed to pieces? Are all your *streams* dry? Jesus is still enough. He has not taken *Himself* from you — and never, never will.

Take your bereaved, stricken and bleeding heart to Him — and rest it upon His heart, which was once bereaved, stricken and bleeding, too! He knows how to bind up the broken heart, to heal the wounded spirit, and to comfort those who mourn.

What is your sorrow?

Has health failed you?

Has property forsaken you?

Have friends turned against you?

Are you tried in your circumstances?

Are you perplexed in your path?

Are providences thickening and darkening around you?

Are you anticipating seasons of approaching trial?

Are you walking in darkness, having no light?

Simply go to Jesus! He is an ever open door — a tender, loving, faithful Friend, ever near. He is a Brother born for your adversity. His grace and sympathy are sufficient for you.

Go to Him in every *trial.* Cast upon Him every *burden.* Take the *infirmity,* the *corruption,* the *cross* as it arises — simply and immediately to Jesus! Jesus is your loving and confiding Brother and Friend, to go to at all times and under all circumstances.

Looking at the world through the cross

Jesus could accomplish man's redemption in no other way than by crucifixion — He must die, and die the death of the cross. What light and glory beam around the cross! Of what prodigies of grace is it the *instrument,* of what glorious truths is it the *symbol,* of what mighty, magic power is it the *source!* Around it, gathers all the light of the Old Testament economy.

It explains every *symbol*;
it substantiates every *shadow*;
it solves every *mystery*;
it fulfills *every type*;
it confirms every *prophecy*
— of that dispensation which had eternally remained unmeaning and inexplicable — except for the death of the Son of God upon the cross!

Not the past only, but *all future splendor* gathers around the cross of our Lord Jesus Christ. It assures us of the ultimate reign of the Savior and tells of the reward which shall spring from His sufferings! And while its one arm points to the divine counsels of eternity *past,* with the other it points to the *future* triumph and glory of Christ's kingdom in the eternity to come. Such is the lowly, yet sublime; the weak, yet mighty instrument — by which the sinner is saved, and God eternally glorified.

The cross of Christ is the grand *consummation* of all preceding dispensations of God to men.

The cross of Christ is the meritorious procuring *cause* of all spiritual blessings to our fallen race.

The cross of Christ is the scene of Christ's splendid *victories* over all His enemies and ours.

The cross of Christ is the most powerful *incentive* to all evangelical holiness.

The cross of Christ is the *instrument* which is to subjugate the world to the supremacy of Jesus.

The cross of Christ is the source of all true peace, joy, and hope.

The cross of Christ is the tree beneath whose shadow all *sin* expired, all *grace* lived!

The cross of our Lord Jesus Christ! What a *holy thrill* these words produce in the heart of those who love the Savior! How significant their *meaning* — how precious their *influence!* Marvelous and irresistible, is the *power* of the cross!

The cross of Christ has subdued many a rebellious will.

The cross of Christ has broken many a marble heart.

The cross of Christ has laid low many a vaunting foe.

The cross of Christ has overcome and triumphed — when all other instruments have failed.

The cross of Christ has transformed the lion-like heart of man, into the lamb-like heart of Christ.

And when lifted up in its own naked simplicity and inimitable grandeur — the cross of Christ has won and attracted millions to its faith, admiration, and love!

What a *marvelous power* does this cross of Jesus possess! It changes the Christian's entire judgment of the *world*. **Looking at the *world* through the *cross*** — his opinion is totally revolutionized. He sees it as it really is — a sinful, empty, vain thing! He learns its *iniquity* — in that it crucified the Lord of life and glory. His *expectations* from the world, his *love* to the world — are changed. He has found another object of love — the Savior whom the world cast out and slew! His love to the world is destroyed by that power which alone could destroy it — the crucifying power of the cross!

It is the cross which eclipses, in the view of the true believer — the glory and attraction of every other object!

What is the *weapon* by which faith combats with, and overcomes the world? What but the cross of Jesus! Just as the natural eye, gazing for a while upon the sun, is blinded for the moment, by its overpowering effulgence to all other objects — so to the believer, concentrating his mind upon the glory of the crucified Savior, studying closely the wonders of *grace* and *love* and *truth* meeting in the cross — the world with all its attraction fades into the full darkness of an eclipse! Christ and His cross are infinitely better than the world and its vanities!

"May I never boast except in the *cross* of our Lord Jesus Christ, through which the *world* has been crucified to me, and I to the world." Galatians 6:14

Bring your sorrows to Me!

"Bring him here to Me." Matthew 17:17

In your moment of disappointment and despair, Jesus meets you with the gracious words, "Bring it here unto Me." And now your spirit revives, your heart bounds, at the words, and you exclaim, "Behold, Lord, I come!"

Jesus says, "**Bring your sorrows to Me!**" Never did the soul find so powerful a *magnet*, attracting to itself affliction in every form, and sorrow in every shade — as Jesus. Standing as in the center of a *world of woe* — He invites every daughter of sorrow, of sin, of grief to repair to Him for support, sympathy, and healing. As the High Priest of His Church for whom alone He suffered, and wept, and sobbed — He unveils a bosom *capacious* enough and *loving* enough, and *sympathizing* enough — to embrace every sufferer, and to pillow every grief. Accept, then, His compassionate invitation, and bring your grief to the soothing, sustaining, sanctifying grace of His heart!

This divine secret!

"Casting all your care upon Him — for He cares for you!" 1 Peter 5:7

How full of soothing and repose are these words! Where, in the world's wilderness, grows the flower of *heart's-ease,* as it blooms and blossoms here!

What *cares* have they lightened!

What *anxieties* have they removed!

What *burdens* have they unclasped!

What springs of *joy* and *comfort* and *hope* have they unsealed in many a sad and oppressed heart!

But do you not, beloved reader, need to be put in constant remembrance of **this divine secret** . . .

of rest, amid toil;

of repose, amid disquietude;

of soothing, amid corroding cares;

of confidence and hope, in the midst of change and troubles?

Bewildered and oppressed by the multitude of anxious thoughts within you — is there not a danger of being so absorbed by the *care* — as to overlook the *Caretaker?* Is there not a *danger* to forget the heart's ease — in the overwhelming of the heart's anxiety?

"Casting all your care upon Him — for He cares for you!"

For me, a poor worthless sinner!

"He Himself bore our sins in His body on the tree, so that we might die to sins and live for righteousness; by His wounds you have been healed." 1 Peter 2:24

Blessed announcement! Not the less hateful, nor hated, is the *sin* because it is forgiven and entirely blotted out. Oh no! Let the Lord touch your heart, Christian reader, with a sense of His pardoning love, with the assurance of His forgiveness — and you will go and hate, and mortify, and forsake it, more resolutely and effectually than ever!

Must the Son of *God* become the Son of *man*, that those who are by nature children of wrath — might become the sons of God! Must God, the eternal God, the high and lofty One, stoop so low as to become incarnate, and that for sinners — **for me, a poor worthless sinner!**

To save *me* from eternal woe — must Jesus suffer, agonize, and die — die in my stead, die for my sins, die an accursed death!

Ah! Lord, what must *sin* be — what must *my* sin be!

How little have I *thought* of it, how little have I *mourned* for it, still less have I *hated* it as I ought to have hated it! Lord, how vile, how unutterably vile I am!

Oh hated sin! Do You forgive it, Father of my mercies? This only makes it more hateful still.

The wrath of God let loose upon His Son!

Divine holiness is best exhibited in the *cross of Jesus. Not hell itself,* as dreadful and eternal as is its suffering — the undying worm, the unquenchable fire, the smoke of the torment that goes up forever and ever — affords such a solemn and impressive spectacle of the *holiness* and *justice* of God in the punishment of sin — as is presented in the death of God's beloved Son!

An eminent Puritan writer thus strikingly puts it,

"Not all the vials of judgment that have or shall be poured out upon this wicked world;

nor the flaming furnace of a sinner's conscience;

nor the irrevocable sentence pronounced against the rebellious devils;

nor the groans of the damned creatures

— give such a demonstration of God's hatred of sin, as **the wrath of God let loose upon His Son!"**

Never did *Divine holiness* appear more beautiful and lovely —

than at the time our Savior's countenance was most marred in the midst of His dying groans. This He Himself acknowledges in that penitential psalm, when God turned His smiling face away from Him, and *thrust His sharp knife of justice into His heart*, which forced that terrible cry from Him, "My God, my God, why have You forsaken Me? Why are You so far from saving Me, so far from the words of My groaning? Yet You are enthroned as the *Holy* One!"

Such an impressive view of God's holiness, the angels in heaven never before beheld — not even when they saw the non-elect spirits hurled from the heights of glory down to the bottomless pit, to be reserved in chains of darkness and woe forever!

Jesus was the *innocent* One, dying for the *guilty* ones — the *holy* One, dying for the *sinful* ones!

Divine *justice*, in its mission of judgment, as it swept by the cross, found the *Son of God impaled* upon its wood beneath the sins and the curse of His people.

Upon Him, its judgment fell;
on His soul, its wrath was poured out;
in His heart, its flaming sword was plunged!

And thus, from Him, *justice* exacted the full penalty of man's transgression — *the last farthing of the great debt!*

Go to the cross, then, my reader, and learn the *holiness* of God. Contemplate the dignity of Christ — His preciousness to His Father's heart — the sinlessness of His nature. And then behold . . .

the sorrow of His soul;
the torture of His body;
the tragedy of His death;
the abasement;
the ignominy;
the humiliation

into the fathomless depths of which the whole transaction plunged our incarnate God!

And let me ask, standing, as you are, before this unparalleled spectacle, "Can you cherish low views of God's holiness, or light views of your own sinfulness?"

He has done all things well!

"He has done all things well!" Mark 7:37

Yes, from first to last, from our cradle to our grave, from the earliest pang of sin's conviction, to the last thrill of sin's forgiveness, from earth to heaven — this will be our testimony in all the way the Lord our God has led us in the wilderness: *"He has done all things well!"*

In *providence* and in *grace,*
in every *truth* of His Word,
in every *lesson* of His love,
in every *stroke* of His rod,
in every *sunbeam* that has shone,
in every *cloud* that has shaded,
in every element that has *sweetened,*
in every ingredient that has *embittered,*
in all that has been mysterious, inscrutable, painful, and humiliating,
in all that He *gave,*
in all that He *took away,*

this testimony is His just due, and this our grateful acknowledgment through time and through eternity: *"He has done all things well!"*

Has He converted us through grace by a way we had thought the most improbable?

Has He torn up all our earthly hopes by the roots?

Has He thwarted our schemes, frustrated our plans, disappointed our expectations?

Has He taught us in schools most trying, by a discipline most severe, and lessons most humbling to our nature?

Has He withered our strength by sickness, reduced us to poverty by loss, crushed our heart by bereavement?

And have we been tempted to exclaim, *"All these things are against me!"*

Ah! no! faith will yet obtain the ascendancy, and sweetly sing:
*"I know in all things that befell,
My Jesus has done all things well!"*
Beloved, it must be so, for Jesus can do nothing wrong!

Study the way of His *providence* and *grace* with the *microscopic eye of faith* — view them in every light, examine them in their minutest detail, as you would the petal of a flower, or the wing of an insect; and, oh, what wonders, what beauty, what marvelous adaptation would you observe in all the varied dealings with you, of your glorious Lord!

A Father's hand!

"My times are in Your hand!" Psalm 31:15
Our times of *adversity* are also in God's hand. As every *sunbeam*

that brightens, so every *cloud* that darkens, comes from God. We are subject to great and sudden reverses in our earthly condition. Joy is often followed by grief; prosperity is often followed by adversity. We are on the pinnacle today; tomorrow at its bottom. Oh! What a change may one event and one moment create! But, beloved, ALL is from the Lord!

Afflictions do not spring from the soil, nor do *troubles* sprout from the ground. *Sorrow* cannot come until God bids it. Until God in His sovereignty permits —

    health cannot fade,
    wealth cannot vanish,
    comfort cannot decay,
    friendship cannot chill, and
    loved ones cannot die.

Your time of sorrow — is *His appointment*. The *bitter cup* which it may please the Lord that you shall drink this year, will not be mixed by *human* hands. In the hand of the Lord, is that cup!

Some *treasure* you are now pressing to your heart — He may ask you to resign.

Some *blessing* you now possess — He may bid you to relinquish.

Some *fond expectation* you now cherish — He may will that you should forego.

Some *lonely path* — He may design that you should tread.

Yes, He may even *bereave* you of all — and yet all, ALL is in His hand! His hand! **A Father's hand**, moving in thick darkness, is shaping every *event*, and arranging every *detail* in your life!

Has *sickness* laid you on a bed of suffering?

Has *bereavement* darkened your home?

Has *adversity* impoverished your resources?

Has *change* lessened your comforts?

Has *sorrow* in one of its many forms crushed your spirit to the earth?

The Lord has done it!

In all that has been *sent*,

in all that has be *recalled*, and

in all that has been *withheld* —

His hand, noiseless and unseen, has brought it about!

Ah! yes, *that hand of changeless love . . .*

    blends a *sweet* with every *bitter*;
    pencils a *bright rainbow* in each *dark cloud*;
    upholds each faltering step;
    shelters within its hollow — and guides with unerring skill, His

chosen people safe to eternal glory!

Dear child of God, your *afflictions*, your *trials*, your *crosses*, your *losses*, your *sorrows* — all, ALL are in **your heavenly Father's hand**, and they cannot come until sent by Him!

Bow that stricken heart! Yield that tempest-tossed soul to His sovereign disposal, to His calm, righteous sway, in the submissive spirit and language of your suffering Savior, "May Your will, O my Father! not mine, be done. My times of sadness and of grief are in Your hand."

Beloved, all is in **your Father's hand!** Be those times what they may:

    times of trial,

    times of temptation,

    times of suffering,

    times of peril,

    times of sunshine or of gloom,

    or times of life or death,

they are in your Father's hand!

Has the Lord seen fit . . .

    to recall some fond blessing,

    to deny some earnest request, or

    painfully to discipline your heart?

All this springs from a Father's love — as fully as though He had unlocked His treasury and poured its costliest gifts at your feet!

All of our times are in our Redeemer's hands! That same Redeemer who carried our *sorrows* in His heart, our *curse* and *sins* on His soul, our *cross* on His shoulder; who died, who rose again, and who lives and intercedes for us, and who will gather all His ransomed around Him in glory — is your Guardian and your Guide! *Your times are in the hands of Him who still bears the print of the nails!*

A soul-satisfying spectacle!

The sight of Jesus is **a soul-satisfying spectacle!**

The *penitent* soul is satisfied, for it sees in Jesus a free pardon of sin.

The *condemned* soul is satisfied, for it receives in Jesus a free justification.

The *believing* soul is satisfied, for it discovers in Jesus a fountain of all grace.

The *tried, tempted, sorrowful* soul is satisfied, for it experiences in Jesus all consolation, sympathy and love.

Oh, what an *all-satisfying Portion* is Jesus!

He satisfies every *holy desire* — for He realizes it.

He satisfies every *craving need* — for He supplies it.

He satisfies every *sore grief* — for He soothes it.

He satisfies the *deepest yearnings, the highest aspirations, the most sublime hopes* of the renewed soul — for all these center and end in Him!

When His beauty is seen

"Yes, He is altogether lovely! This is my Beloved, and this is my Friend!" Song of Songs 5:16

O what a Savior is Jesus Christ! He is the chief among ten thousand! Look at His sinless, yet real humanity — without a single taint, yet sympathizing with us in all our various conditions — our afflictions — our temptations — our infirmities — our griefs. Now that He is in glory, He is still cherishing a brother's heart, bending down His ear to our petitions — ever standing near . . .

　　to catch our sighs,

　　to dry our tears,

　　to provide for our needs,

　　to guide us by His counsel, and

　　afterwards to receive us to glory!

O what a Savior is Jesus Christ! When He is known — all other beings are eclipsed.

When His beauty is seen — all other beauty fades. When His love is felt — He becomes supremely enthroned in the affections.

To know Him more, becomes the one desire of the renewed mind; and to make Him more known, is the one aim of the Christian life. O what a Savior is Jesus Christ!

Your Almighty Friend!

"Yes, He is altogether lovely! This is my Beloved, and this is my Friend!" Song of Songs 5:16

Because Jesus is the Almighty God — His people have an Almighty Burden-Bearer.

We are a *burdened* people. Every believer carries a burden peculiar to himself. *What is your burden, O believer?*

Is it indwelling sin?

Is it some natural infirmity of the flesh?

Is it a constitutional weakness?

Is it some domestic trial?

Is it a personal or relative trial?

Is it the loss of property?

Is it the decay of health?

Is it soul anxiety?

Is it mental despondency?

Come, oppressed and burdened believer, ready to give up all and sink! Behold Jesus, the Almighty God, omnipotent to *transfer your burden to Himself,* and give you rest! It is well that you are sensible of the pressure — that you feel your weakness and insufficiency — and that you are brought to the end of all your own power. Now turn to **your Almighty Friend**, who is the Creator of the ends of the earth — the everlasting God, who does not faint, neither is weary.

Oh, what strength there is in Jesus for the weak, and faint, and drooping of His flock! You are ready to succumb to your foes, and you think the battle of faith is lost. Cheer up! Jesus, your Savior, friend, and brother — is the Almighty God, and will perfect *His strength* in your weakness. The battle is not yours, but His! Jesus . . .

sustains our *infirmities,*

bears our *burdens,*

supplies our *needs,* and

encircles us with the shield of His Almightiness!

What a Divine spring of consolation and strength to the tired and afflicted saint, is the Almightiness of Jesus. Your *sorrow* is too deep — your *affliction* too heavy — your *difficulty* too great for any mere human to resolve. It distances in its intensity and magnitude, the sympathy and the power of man.

Come, you who are tempest-tossed and not comforted. Come, you whose spirit is wounded, whose heart is broken, whose mind is bowed down to the dust. Hide for a little while within *Christ's sheltering Almightiness!* Jesus is equal to your condition.

His *strength* is almighty!

His *love* is almighty!

His *grace* is almighty!

His *sympathy* is almighty!

His *arm* is almighty!

His *resources* are infinite, fathomless, measureless!

And all this Almightiness is on your side, and will bring you through the fire and through the water.

Almighty to *rescue* — He is also your Brother and Friend to *sympathize*. And while His Divine arm encircles, upholds, and keeps you — His human soul, touched with the feeling of your infirmities, yearns over you with all the deep intensity of its compassionate tenderness!

"Yes, He is altogether lovely! This is my Beloved, and this is my Friend!" Song of Songs 5:16

Christ must be all!

We cannot keep our eye too exclusively or too intently fixed on Jesus. All salvation is *in* Him. All salvation proceeds *from* Him. All salvation leads *to* Him. And for the assurance and comfort of our salvation, we are to repose believingly and entirely on Him. **Christ must be all!** Christ the *beginning* — Christ the *center* — and Christ the *end*.

Oh sweet truth — to you who are sensible of your poverty, vileness, and insufficiency, and of the ten thousand flaws and failures of which, perhaps, no one is cognizant but God and your own soul! Oh, to turn and rest in Christ — a *full* Christ — a *loving* Christ — a *tender* Christ, whose heart's love never chills, from whose eye darts no reproof, from whose lips breathes no sentence of condemnation! **Christ must be all!**

As though it had never been!

Beloved, soon, O how soon! all that now loads the heart with care, and wrings it with sorrow — all that dims the eye with tears, and renders the day anxious and the night sleepless — will be **as though it had never been!** Emerging from the entanglement, the dreariness, the solitude, the loneliness, and the temptations of the wilderness — you shall enter upon your everlasting rest, your unfading inheritance, where there is no sorrow, no declension, no sin, no sunset, no twilight, no evening shadows, no midnight darkness! But all is one perfect, cloudless, eternal day — for Jesus is the joy, the light, and the glory thereof!

What is heaven?

Beloved, **what is heaven?** What is the final glory of the saints? Is it not the best place, the richest inheritance provided by the Father for the people ransomed and brought home to glory by

His Son? Heaven is a place designated by God, chosen and consecrated by Him for the people redeemed by the precious blood of
His dear Son. And when we enter there, we shall enter as children
welcomed to a Father's home! It will be the best that God can give
us! He will bestow upon us, who deserved the least — the best in
His power to bestow:

the best Savior,
the best robe,
the best banquet,
the best inheritance.

In heaven, there will be . . .
nothing more to taint,
nothing more to sully,
nothing more to embitter,
nothing more to wound,
no serpent to beguile,
no Eve to ensnare,
no spoiler to destroy,
no sin to defile,
no adversity to sadden,
no misunderstanding to alienate,
no tongue to defame,
no suspicion to chill,
no tear,
nor sickness,
nor death,
nor parting.

It will be the best part of the pure, radiant, glorified universe
which God will assign to His people! Saints of the Most High!

Let the prospect cheer, sanctify, and comfort you! It will not be
long that you are to labor and battle here on earth. It is but a *little
while* that you are to occupy your present sphere of conflict, of
trial, and of sorrow. The time is coming — oh, how fast it speeds!
Soon the Lord Jesus Christ will bring you home to heaven!

"In My Father's house are many rooms; I am going there to prepare a place for you. And if I go and prepare a place for you, I will
come back and take you to be with Me — that you also may be
where I am!" John 14:2-3

Oh encouraging truth!

"I the Lord search the heart!" Jeremiah 17:10

Solemn as is this view of the Divine character — the believing mind finds in it sweet and hallowed repose. What more consolatory truth in some of the most trying positions of a child of God than this — *the Lord knows the heart!* The *world* condemns us, and the *saints* may wrongly judge us — but *God* knows the heart! And to those who have been led into deep discoveries of their heart's hidden evil, to whom have been made startling and distressing unveilings — how precious is this character of God, "I the Lord search the heart."

Is there a single *recess* of our hearts we would veil from His penetrating glance? Is there a *corruption* we would hide from His view? Is there an *evil* of which we would have Him ignorant? Oh no! Mournful and humiliating as is the spectacle, we would throw open every door, and uplift every window, and invite and urge His scrutiny and inspection, making no concealments, and indulging in no reserves, and framing no excuses when dealing with the great Searcher of hearts, exclaiming, "Search me, O God, and know my heart; test me and know my anxious thoughts. Point out anything in me that offends you, and lead me along the path of everlasting life."

And while the Lord is thus acquainted with the evil of our hearts, He most graciously *conceals that evil from the eyes of others.* He seems to say, by His benevolent conduct, "I see My child's infirmity." Then, covering it with His hand, exclaims, "but no other eye shall see it, but my own!" Oh, the touching tenderness, the lovingkindness of our God! Knowing, as He does, all the evil of our nature, He yet veils that evil from every human eye — that others may not despise us as we often despise ourselves. Who but God, could *know* it? Who but God, would *conceal* it?

And how blessed, too, to remember that while God knows all the *evil*, He is as intimately acquainted with all the *good* that is in the hearts of His people! He knows all that His Spirit has implanted — all that His grace has wrought. **Oh encouraging truth!**

That spark of love, faint and flickering;

that pulsation of life, low and tremulous;

that touch of faith, feeble and hesitating;

that groan, that sigh;

that low thought of self that leads a man to seek the shadows;

that self-abasement that places his mouth in the dust;

oh, not one of these sacred emotions is unseen, unnoticed by God! *His eye ever rests with infinite compassion and delight on His own image in the renewed soul.*

Your present adversity

"And we know that all things work together for good to those who love God, to those who are the called according to His purpose." Romans 8:28

It is palpably clear and emphatically true, that all that occurs in the Lord's government of His people conspires for, and works out, and results in, their highest happiness and their greatest good. The gloomiest and most painful circumstances in the history of the child of God, without a solitary exception — are all conspiring, and all working together, for his real and permanent good.

The painful and inexplicable dispensations, which at the present moment may be thickening and deepening around your path, are but so many *mysteries in God's government,* which He is working out to their certain, satisfactory, and happy results. And when the good thus embosomed in the lowering cloud of some crushing providence, accomplishes its benevolent and heaven-sent mission, then trial will expand its dark pinions and fly away — and sorrow will roll up its somber drapery and disappear!

All things, under the government of an infinitely great, all-wise, righteous, and beneficent Lord God, work together for good. What that good may be — the *shape* it may assume — the *complexion* it may wear — the *end* to which it may be subservient — we cannot tell. *To our dim view* it may appear an evil — but to God's far seeing eye it is a positive good. Oh, truth most divine! Oh, words most consolatory!

How many whose *eye* traces this page, it may be whose *tears* bedew it, whose *sighs* breathe over it, whose *prayers* hallow it — may be wading in deep waters, may be drinking bitter cups, and are ready to exclaim, "All these things are *against* me!" Oh no, beloved of God — all these things are *for* you! Do not be afraid! Christ restrains the flood upon whose heaving bosom He serenely sits. Christ controls the waters, whose sounding waves obey the mandate of His voice. Christ's cloudy chariot is paved with love! Then, fear not! Your Father grasps the helm of your storm-tossed vessel — and through cloud and tempest, will steer it safely to the port of endless rest!

Will it not be a real good, if your present adversity results . . .
in the dethronement of some worshiped idol?
in the endearing of Christ to your soul?
in the closer conformity of your mind to God's image?
in the purification of your heart?

in your more thorough fitness for heaven?

in a revival of God's work within you?

in stirring you up to more prayer?

in enlarging your heart to all that love the same Savior?

in stimulating you to increased activity for the conversion of sinners, for the diffusion of the truth, and for the glory of God?

Oh yes! good, real good, permanent good must result from all the Divine dispensations in your history.

Bitter repentance, shall end in the experienced sweetness of Christ's love.

The *festering wound,* shall but elicit the healing balm.

The *overpowering burden,* shall but bring you to the tranquil rest.

The *storm,* shall but quicken your footsteps to the Hiding Place.

The bitter-cold north wind and the balmy south wind, shall breathe together over your garden — and the spices shall flow out.

In a little while — oh, how soon! you shall pass away from earth to heaven, and in its clearer, serener light shall read the truth, often read with tears before, "And we know that all things work together for good to those who love God, to those who are the called according to His purpose."

The little things of life

"But even the very hairs of your head are all numbered." Luke 12:7

You know so little of God, my reader, because you live at such a distance from God. You have . . .

so little communion with Him,

so little confession of sin,

so little searching of your own conscience,

so little probing of your own heart,

so little transaction with Him in **the little things of life**. You deal with God in *great* matters. You take great trials to God, great perplexities, great needs; but in the minutiae of each day's history, in what are called the *little* things of life — you have no dealings with God whatever — and consequently you know so little of the *love,* so little of the *wisdom,* so little of the *glory,* of your resplendent covenant God and reconciled Father.

I tell you, the man who lives with God in *little matters* — who walks with God in the *minutiae* of his life — is the man who becomes the best acquainted with God — with His character, His faithfulness, His love. To meet God in my *daily trials,* to take to

Him the trials of my calling, the trials of my church, the trials of my family, the trials of my own heart; to take to Him that which brings the shadow upon my brow, which rends the sigh from my heart — to remember it is not too trivial to take to God — above all, to take to Him the least taint upon the conscience, the slightest pressure of sin upon the heart, the softest conviction of departure from God — to take it to Him, and confess it at the foot of the cross, with the hand of faith upon the bleeding sacrifice — oh! these are the paths in which a man becomes intimately and closely acquainted with God!

All dropping from the outstretched, munificent hand of a loving, gracious, and bountiful Father!

Beloved, remember that all our past and all our coming prosperity, if indeed He shall so appoint it — is in the hand of God.

It is His *wisdom* that suggests our plans,
it is His *power* that guides, and
it is His *goodness* that makes them successful.
Every flower that blooms in our path,
every smile that gladdens it,
every mercy that bedews it,
comes to us from our heavenly Father.

Oh! for grace to recognize God in all our mercies!
How much sweeter will be our sweets,
how much more blessed our blessings,
how   much   more   endeared   our   endearments
— to see them **all dropping from the outstretched, munificent hand of a loving, gracious, and bountiful Father!** Oh! for a heart lifted up in holy returns of love, gratitude and praise!

That most excellent and superlative knowledge!

There is everything we need in Jesus to endear His name to our hearts.

He is our *Prophet*, teaching us the will of the Father.

He is our *Priest*, offering up Himself as our atoning Victim.

He is our *King*, erecting His throne in our hearts, and subduing us to Himself as His loving and obedient subjects.

He is our *Friend*, loving us at all times.

He is our *Brother*, bone of our bone, and flesh of our flesh, born for our adversity.

He is our Great High *Priest*, touched with the feeling of our infirmities, tempted in all points as we are — and in our sorrows, griefs, and trials encircling us with the many-folded robe of His tender, loving sympathy.

O to know Jesus — **that most excellent and superlative knowledge!** With Paul we may well count all things but loss for its possession. To know Him as the *Savior* — to know Him as our *Friend* — to know Him as our *Brother* — to know Him as our *Advocate* — to know Him as our *Portion*, is endless life and glory!

The altogether lovely one!

With what pen, dipped though it were in heaven's brightest hues, can we portray the image of Jesus?

The perfection of our Lord was the perfection of *holiness*. His Deity, essential holiness; His humanity without sin, the impersonation of holiness. All that He *was, said,* and *did* — was as flashes of holiness emanating from the fountain of essential purity, and kindling their dazzling and undying radiance around each step He trod. How *humble*, too, His character! How holy the thoughts He breathed, how pure the words He spoke, how gentle the spirit He exemplified, how tender and sympathizing the outgoings of His compassion and love to man. He is the chief among ten thousand, **the altogether lovely one!**

The chief object of your study

We *know* so much of divine truth, my reader, as we have in a measure a personal *experience* of it in our souls. The mere *speculatist* and *notionalist* in religion is as unsatisfactory and unprofitable as the mere theorist and declaimer in science. For all practical purposes, both are but *ciphers.*

The character and the degree of our spiritual knowledge, begins and terminates in our knowledge of Christ. Christ is the test of its reality — the measure of its depth — and the source of its growth.

If you are advancing in an experimental, sanctifying acquaintance with the Lord Jesus, you are advancing in that knowledge which Paul thus estimates, "I count all things but loss for the excellency of the knowledge of Christ Jesus my Lord." Dear reader, let **the chief object of your study** be to know the Lord Jesus. It may be in the region of your sinfulness, emptiness, weakness, and foolishness — that you learn Him. Nevertheless, however humiliating the school, slow the progress, and limited the attainment, count every fresh step you make in a personal acquaintance with the Lord Jesus — as a nobler triumph, and as bringing you into the possession of more real wealth than were the whole chests of human knowledge and science mastered, and its untold treasures poured at your feet!

When *adversity* comes — when *death* approaches — when *eternity* unveils — oh! how indescribably valuable, how inconceivably precious will then be one faith's touch, one faith's glimpse of a crucified and risen Savior! All other attainments then vanish, and the only knowledge that abides, soothes, and comforts — is a heartfelt acquaintance with the most sublime fact of the Gospel — that Jesus came into the world to save sinners. Oh! Whatever other studies may engage your thoughts, do not forget, as you value your eternal destiny, to *study the Lord Jesus Christ!*

Deeper knowledge of Jesus

Cultivate frequent and devout contemplations of *the glory of Christ.* Immense will be the benefit accruing to your soul. The mind thus preoccupied, filled, and expanded, will be enabled to present a stronger resistance to the ever advancing and insidious encroachments of the world. No place will be found for vain thoughts, and no desire or time for carnal enjoyments. Oh, how *crucifying* and *sanctifying* are clear views of the glory of Emmanuel! *How emptying, humbling, and abasing!* With the *patriarch*, we then exclaim, "I abhor myself, and repent in dust and ashes." And with the *prophet*, "Woe is me! for I am undone; because I am a man of unclean lips, for my eyes have seen the King, the Lord Almighty." And with the *apostle*, "But God forbid that I should glory, save in the cross of our Lord Jesus Christ, by whom the world is crucified unto me, and I unto the world."

Oh, then, aim to get your mind filled with enlarged and yet expanding views of the glory of the Redeemer. Let it, in all the discoveries it affords of the Divine mind and majesty, be the one subject of your thoughts — the one theme of your conversation. Place no *limit* to your knowledge of Christ. Ever consider that you have but read the *preface* to the volume; you have but touched the *fringe* of the sea. Stretching far away beyond you, are undiscovered beauties, and precious views, and sparkling glories — each encouraging your advance, inviting your research, and asking the homage of your faith, the tribute of your love, and the dedication of your life.

Go forward, then! The glories that yet must be revealed to you in a growing knowledge of Jesus — what imagination can conceive, what pen can describe them? Jesus stands ready to unveil all the beauties of His person; and to admit you into the very pavilion of His love. There is not a chamber of His heart that He will not throw open to you — not a blessing that He will not bestow upon you — not a glory that He will not show to you.

You shall see greater things than you have yet seen:

greater depths of your *sin* shall be revealed,

deeper sense of the cleansing efficacy of the atoning blood shall be felt,

clearer views of your acceptance in the Beloved,

greater discoveries of God's love, and

greater depths of grace and glory in Jesus shall be enjoyed.

Your communion with God shall be closer, and more the fruit of adopting love in your heart. Your feet shall be as hinds' feet, and you shall walk on high places. Your peace shall flow as a river, and your righteousness as the waves of the sea.

Sorrow shall wound you less deeply,

affliction shall press you less heavily,

tribulation shall affect you less keenly,

all this, and infinitely more, will result from your **deeper knowledge of Jesus**.

The astonishing, the marvelous love!

The cross of Jesus, inspires our love to Him. It would seem impossible to be brought by the Holy Spirit to the foot of the cross, and not feel the *inspiration of love.* Surely a believing apprehension of the *amazing,* the *unparalleled* love of Jesus, bending His look of forgiveness upon us from the cross — will thaw our icy hearts into the warmest glow of affection. Believe that Jesus loves you — and your heart shall glow with a love in return which will bear it on in a willing obedience and unreserved surrender, in faithful service and patient suffering, enwrapped, consumed amid the flames of its own heaven *inspired* and heaven *ascending* affection. **The astonishing, the marvelous love**, He has exhibited in giving you His beloved Son to die in your stead — are *cords* by which He would draw your loving heart to Himself!

Because He loved her!

Jesus sustains no association to His Church more expressive, than that of the *marriage* relationship. From all eternity, He forever *betrothed* her to Himself. He asked for her at the hands of her Father — and the Father gave her to Him. He entered into a covenant that she would be His. The conditions of that covenant were great, but not too great for His love to undertake. They were, that He should assume her nature, discharge her legal obligations, endure her punishment, repair her ruin, and bring her to glory! He undertook all, and He accomplished all — **because He loved her!** The love of Jesus to His Church, is the love of the most tender husband. It is single, constant, affectionate, matchless, wonderful. Jesus . . . sympathizes with her,

nourishes her,

provides for her,

clothes her,

watches over her, and

indulges her with the most intimate and endearing tenderness!

Eternally repose your weary soul in the bosom of Jesus!

Forward, believer in Christ, to the toils, duties, and trials of another stage of life's journey! Jesus is enough for them all. Jesus will be with you in them all. Jesus will triumphantly conduct you through them all.

Beloved one, live in the constant expectation of soon seeing Jesus face to face — conversing with He whom here below, cheered, comforted, and sweetened many a weary step of your Christian pilgrimage. That moment is speeding on. In a little while and all that now wounds and ruffles, tempts and pollutes — will have disappeared like the foam upon the billow, and you shall **eternally repose your weary soul in the bosom of Jesus!**

The solitary object of His love!

It is a great mercy when we can retire from the crowd and deal with God individually — when we can take the precious promises to ourselves individually — when we can repair to Jesus with individual sins, infirmities, and sorrows — feeling that His *eye* bends its glance upon us — His *ear* bows down to us — His *hand* is outstretched to us — His whole *heart* absorbed in us as though not another petitioner or sufferer offered a request, or unveiled a sorrow. As if, in a word, we were **the solitary object of His love!**

His invitation to you is, "Come unto Me." He would have you come. You cannot honor Him more than by . . .

recognizing His personal relation to yourself,

disclosing your personal circumstances,

making personal confession of personal sin,

presenting personal needs, and unveiling personal infirmities, backslidings, and sorrows!

That friend!

"There is a friend who sticks closer than a brother." Proverbs 18:24

The power of human sympathy is amazing — if it leads the heart to Christ. It is paralyzed — if it leads only to ourselves. Oh, how feeble and inadequate are we to administer to a diseased mind, to heal a broken heart, to strengthen the feeble hand, and to confirm the trembling knees! Our mute sympathy, our prayerful silence — is often the best exponent of our affection, and the most effectual expression of our aid.

But if, taking the object of our solicitude by the hand, we gently lead him to God — if we conduct him to Jesus, portraying to his view the depth of His love, the perfection of His atoning work, the sufficiency of His grace, His readiness to pardon, His power to save, the exquisite sensibility of His nature, and thus His perfect sympathy with every human sorrow — we have then most truly and most effectually soothed the sorrow, healed the wound, and strengthened the hand in God.

There is no sympathy, no love, no gentleness, no tenderness, no patience, like Christ's! Oh how sweet, how encouraging — to know that Jesus sympathetically enters into my afflictions — my temptations — my sorrows — my joys. May this truth endear Him to our souls! May it constrain us to unveil our whole heart to Him, in the fullest confidence of the closest, most sacred, and precious friendship. May it urge us to do those things always which are most pleasing in His sight.

Beloved, never forget — let these words linger upon your ear, as the echoes of music that never die — in all your sorrows, in all your trials, in all your needs, in all your assaults, in all your conscious wanderings, in life, in death, and at the day of judgment — you possess a friend that sticks closer than a brother! **That friend** is Jesus!

"Yes, He is altogether lovely! This is my Beloved, and this is my Friend!" Song of Songs 5:16

CONSIDER JESUS

Thoughts for Daily Duty, Service, and Suffering

Consider Jesus—in Lowliness of Birth

"Is not this the carpenter's son?" —Matthew 13:55

What a remarkable fact in the history of Jesus does this question, asked with mingled surprise and contempt, betray! It presents Him in a point of light in which, perhaps, few have paused to study Him, and yet than which there is scarcely another more real and instructive. It invites us to consider Jesus as the Son of man, as the son of a carpenter, and in all probability, until He began to be about thirty years of age, assisting Joseph in his humble calling. Hence it was asked concerning Jesus, "Is not this the *carpenter?*" How truly did the Son of God identify Himself with the humanity and the curse He came to ransom and remove. And when we see those hands which built the universe building earthly dwellings for man—squaring the beam, plying the saw, thrusting the plane, driving the nail, constructing and raising the framework—we behold personally Him tasting the bitterness of that part of the curse which enjoined, "In the sweat of your face shall you eat bread."

We learn from this that, obscurity of birth and lowliness of craft are no dishonor to him whose condition it may be; and that they have often been found in alliance with true greatness of character, high devotedness to God, noble and useful deeds for man. God, who is no respecter of people, looks upon man's outward estate with a very different eye to that with which the world looks upon it. You ask for the proof. Behold, the Incarnate Son of God, instead of selecting, as He might have done, a princess for His mother and a palace for His birth, lo! His reputed father is a carpenter, His mother, though of royal lineage, is too poor to present on the day of her purification an offering more costly than "a pair of turtledoves," and the scene of His wondrous advent is among the beasts of the field feeding quietly at their troughs.

But, consider Him. You are, perhaps, taunted for your obscure birth, looked down upon for your humble calling, slighted for your social position, and are discouraged from any attempt to rise above it and strike out a path of wider influence and nobler exertion. But learn from Jesus that there is no dishonor in humble parentage, that true dignity belongs to honest toil, and that personal piety, consecration to God, and far-reaching usefulness to man, may be closely associated with those whose niche in society is low in the scale, and whose walk through life is along its more shaded and secluded pathway.

We have referred to LABOR. Here, again, Jesus demands our consideration. Our Divine Savior might be termed, in modern parlance, a 'working man.' He was, in early life, a *carpenter.* Labor was concurrent with man's creation. Before the fall, God sent him into the garden to keep it. And although the ground brought forth spontaneously, yet it was beneath his culturing hand that the earth was to bloom and blossom as the rose. Idleness was no part of our original constitution; God never intended that man's powers should be stunted, and that his life should evaporate in useless and ignoble repose. Be up, then, and doing. Be ready for any labor, prepared for any duty, willing for any sacrifice, active, honest, and earnest in any and every sphere in which God may place you.

Consider Jesus! He knows your walk. He will sympathize with, and give you grace for, the difficulties and discouragements, the temptations and trials, peculiar to your position in life. And however obscure your birth, or lowly your calling, or cramped your powers, strive to imitate, please, and glorify Him. Not totally hidden will then your light be. Your trust in God, your resemblance to Christ, the example of your honest industry, patient endurance and virtuous bearing—which poverty could not crush or obscurity veil—will influence for good all whose privilege it may be to know, admire, and love you. Thus your "light will shine out of obscurity," and, humble though your course and limited though your sphere may have been, you will not have lived for God and for man in vain.

Consider Jesus—in the Elevation of Rank *"King of kings, and Lord of lords."*—Revelation 19:16

The twofold nature of Jesus brought Him into the closest personal relation to, and sympathy with, the two great divisions of the race—the Commonalty and the Nobility—and thus He becomes a proper subject of instructive study to both. We have considered His obscurity and abasement as man; it remains that we study Him as possessing the highest rank and as wearing the noblest title as God— *"KING of kings, and LORD of lords."* The present reflection, therefore, addresses itself to those upon whom is conferred the honor, the duties, and the responsibilities of high birth and rank. It is not often that such are especially selected by the ministers of religion as objects of pious instruction. For every other class Christian sympathy is felt, and religious efforts made; while those of higher caste in society are passed by in cold neglect, as if their eternal interests were not equally as precious, and as if their soul-perils were not transcendently greater. But what are the godly instructions we may gather from a consideration of Jesus in the light of His elevated rank?

The first that impresses us is that, human rank is of Divine appointment.

Every privilege of nobility originates with God. *"He puts down one, and raises up another."* Human society in its framework manifests His molding hand. It is impossible to trace the various grades which exist, the dependent relation of each to the other, and of all to God, and not admire His wisdom and adore His goodness in the marvelous construction of societies. To Him, then, you are to refer your rank. Whether by inheritance, or by privilege, you are bound to acknowledge God in its bestowment, seriously pondering the end for which it was given, the responsibilities it involves, the duties it imposes, and the solemn account you have to give of its use at the last Great Day.

Consider Jesus as on no occasion either denying or renouncing His rank. On the contrary, at the very moment that He was engaged in the most condescending act of His life He asserted it. *"I, your LORD and MASTER, have washed your feet."* It has been the mistaken idea of some good men that, conversion to Christ imperatively demanded and necessarily involved a relinquishment of their social position. No judgment could be more at fault, no step more unscriptural. The religion of Christ *levels* and destroys nothing but ungodliness and error. The Bible teaching is, *"Let every man abide in the calling wherein he was called."* If, then, the grace of God has called you in the higher walks of life, ennobled and titled, to relinquish your position and, consequently, its moral influence in the Church and in the world, were a folly and a sin. Providence and Grace never clash. Where Grace has called you, there let Providence keep you, and use you for God.

Consider Jesus in the humility and condescension which rank imposes. Was there ever a being so high, and yet ever one so meek and lowly, as Christ?

Watch against the arrogance of high birth. The costliest and brightest gem in your coronet will be the humility with which you wear it. *"Condescend to men of low estate." "Learn of Me, for I am meek and lowly in heart."*

Consider Jesus as consecrating His rank to the good of man and the glory of God. See that yours is not selfishly possessed, but magnanimously employed. Wear it not as a mere adornment, but use it as a mighty power, capable of conferring elevation, prosperity, and happiness upon all who are privileged to come within the warmth and glow of its sunshine. Keep the impressive fact full in view that, at Jesus' feet every princely diadem, and sacred mitre, and noble coronet, and ermined robe must be laid, and into His hands the stewardship be surrendered! Lay your title at His feet *now*—a holy and a consecrated thing to God! Under a solemn sense of its dreadful responsibility, seek grace from Christ to devote it to the increase of His kingdom, the furtherance of His gospel, and the well-being of man in the world.

Consider Jesus—in the Possession of Wealth *"He was RICH."*—2 Cor. 8:9

Rank and wealth may exist apart from each other. In Jesus they were combined. He could not be the Divinest, and not be the Richest Being in the universe; the Creator, and not the Owner of all worlds. Moreover, He could say, *"All SOULS are mine"*—a wealth second only to the affluence of His own absolute Godhead. Thus He becomes a study for the wealthy—a study for a *rich Christian*—oppressed with the anxieties, exposed to the snares, armed with the power, and speeding to the final Judgment laden with the fearful responsibilities and the solemn account of WEALTH! But, 'Consider Him.'

Jesus ascribed His wealth to God. While asserting essential Deity, He ever acknowledged His dependence upon His Father as the Mediator and Redeemer of man. In this light we interpret His remarkable declaration—

"The Son can do nothing of Himself but what He sees the Father do." "As the Father has life in Himself, so has He given to the Son to have life in Himself." Thus consider Him! To God you owe, and to God you are bound to ascribe, your wealth. Your own efforts and skill had been a failure, disappointing and ruinous, but for His enriching blessing. Say not in your heart, *"My power and the might of mine hand has gotten me this wealth. But you shall remember the*

Lord your God: for it is HE that gives you power to get wealth." Do you thus give God the glory? And as you survey your broad acres, and count your treasured gold, and speculate on your profitable investments, do you in your heart gratefully and devoutly acknowledge, "I owe all this to God! Not my hand, nor my skill, nor my toil, but to Your favor, help, and blessing, O Lord, alone I attribute it?"

Jesus, though rich, was destitute of the PRIDE of wealth. Human pride is one of the most operative causes of self-destruction—and wealth is its prolific parent. "Behold," says God to Jerusalem, "this was the iniquity of your sister Sodom, *pride and fullness of bread."* The poor are often oppressed with a sense of their insignificance, but the rich are prone to be inflated and self- important, "pride"— *purse-pride*—"compassing them about as a chain." Rejoice if Divine grace has taught you your spiritual poverty, nothingness, and vileness, so enabling you to walk humbly with God in your wealth. "Let the *rich* rejoice in that he is *made low:"*—laid low beneath the cross—"because as the flower of the grass he shall pass away."

Jesus was free from the WORLDLINESS of wealth. The rich are peculiarly exposed to the world. The means which they possess of surrounding themselves with its pomp and show, its luxury and pleasures, are a terrible snare, which the grace of God alone can conquer. Study Jesus! With the world at His command, how unworldly! From not thus studying and imitating Him, many a wealthy professor has made shipwreck of his faith, character, and usefulness, swept away by the irresistible force of *unsanctified* riches. "Demas has forsaken me, *having loved this present world."* Oh! beware of the world!

Your "riches will become corrupt, your gold and your silver cankered, and their rust shall be a witness against you," if they plunge you into the temptations, covetousness, and sins of this present evil world!

Jesus devoted His riches to the glory of God. Is your wealth thus devoted? Is

"Holiness to the Lord" impressed upon your coin? Whose superscription does it bear? Christ has poor brethren needing help. His cause languishes from lack of support. His devoted, faithful ministers, many of them, are toiling amid straitness and pinching poverty. Oh, liberally scatter your wealth, and as you lay it down at the feet of Jesus, exclaim with lowliness and gratitude,

"Of *Your own* have I given You, dearest Lord!" Thus cultivating a generous liberality, watching against the temptations of riches, and keeping in full view the solemn account of your stewardship, let your constant, earnest prayer be—"In all times of our WEALTH, good Lord, deliver us!"

Consider Jesus—in the Straitness of Poverty *"He became poor."*— 2 Cor. 8:9

The *wealth* of Jesus, of which we have already spoken, was *essential;* His *poverty,* of which we are now to speak, was willingly *assumed.* "He became poor." By an act of unparalleled beneficence, He emptied Himself of His wealth and linked Himself with a life of dependent poverty. The only riches He retained—and these

He scattered with a profuse and unbounded generosity—were the 'unsearchable riches of His grace', bestowed indiscriminately and freely upon the vilest of the race. So poor was He, holy women ministered to Him of their substance; and so homeless, the foxes had holes, and the birds of the air nests, but He, the Creator of the world, had not where to lay His head! "Consider Him."

We learn, in the first place, that poverty may exist in alliance with greatness and moral wealth. There is nothing in poverty essentially degrading or demoralizing. Wealth, unsanctified by Divine grace, may depress our moral instincts, vitiate and impair our noblest faculties, developing and arming, to an almost unbounded extent, the innate evil of our nature; but poverty, hallowed of God, has often proved a school of grace in which that same nature has been molded into a vessel of honor, penciled with the beauty of holiness, sanctified and made fit for Christ's service.

Thus, poverty is not essentially sinful, though springing from original sin, and is often the sad and bitter fruit of willful transgression against the soul and God—improvidence, indolence, and intemperance, entailing poverty and need, misery and woe. Yet, as in the case of our adorable Lord, and in countless instances of His disciples, it may be allied to the highest intellectual development, to the richest spiritual grace, and to the noblest formation of character. Did there ever exist one so poor in this world, yet one so holy, so gracious, and so useful as Jesus? Learn of Him, then, who stamped with so great a dignity, and invested with so rich a luster, a life of virtuous poverty and need, before which the worth and glitter of unsanctified riches fade into insignificance.

Straitened circumstances aid in the development of a life of faith in God. Such was the life of Jesus. As man, He as much lived by faith on God as His disciples. He never bids us walk in a path divergent from His own, but in each one *"left us an example that we should follow His steps."* Thus the poor are dependent upon God, and the poverty of the Christian—often his greatest wealth—leads him to prayer, and prayer brings him into closer acquaintance with God, and the more he knows of the character of God, the more he learns to love and fear and trust in Him. *"The life I now live in the flesh, I live by the faith of the Son of God."* Oh, take your poverty to God. Your Heavenly Father knows and is pledged, has promised and is able, to supply all your needs. Do you think that He who feeds the birds of the air will neglect the children of His love? Never! Oh, how your very poverty may enrich you in prayer, faith, and grace! Sweet to live a life of childlike dependence upon God!

To know and feel, "My Father thinks for, and takes care of, me."

The poverty of Jesus was the wealth of others. Thus there are none, so straitened and tried in their circumstances, who may not contribute, in some degree, to the temporal or the spiritual necessities of others. *"As poor, yet making many rich."* Hence we often find in the poor the greatest sympathy and help for the poor. Let not your limited resources, then, be a veil for stinginess; your poverty an excuse for unkindness. But imitate the early Christians, whose *"deep poverty abounded unto the riches of their liberality;"* and consider Jesus, *"who, though He was rich, yet for our sakes became poor, that we through His poverty might be made rich."* Be submissive to God's will in poverty. LET CHRIST BE YOUR SOUL'S PORTION. Lay up treasures in heaven. And let your life, amid its toil and trial, its poverty and need, be a holy preparation for your riches of glory above. *"Trust in the Lord, and do good; so shall you dwell in the land, and verily you shall be fed."*

Consider Jesus—in the Exercise of Influence *"Be followers of me, even as I am of Christ."*—1 Cor. 11:1

INFLUENCE is the subject which these words suggest for our present meditation—the influence of Christ reflected in the influence of the Christian.

"Follow me, as I follow Christ." The power of influencing others is a wonderful and responsible gift of God. Every individual possesses it. Unknown though his name, and obscure though his sphere may be, he is the center of a circle touching at every point for good or for evil all who come within the radius of his moral power—the potency of which cannot be measured, the results of which can never be fully known.

No person is absolutely neutral in this life—none so humble as not to take hold on the vitalities of some individual's inner being, thoughts, and feelings. High or low, rich or poor, we throw off from us, and we receive in return, trains of influences which shape the opinions, mold the characters, and determine the destinies, both of ourselves and others. We may not be able to explain the nature or estimate the results of this law; nevertheless, in the last great day the truth will flash upon us with startling effect— *"No man lives to himself."* The question once defiantly and insultingly asked of God, *"Am I my brother's keeper?"* will be answered with a Divine affirmative crushing as thunder, or thrilling as music,— "You *were!* and you have *ruined* him forever by your ungodly example," or, "You have *saved* him forever by your holy influence!" How solemn this truth! It is this power of action and reaction—this reciprocity of moral influences—which gives a character, reality, and responsibility to all our thoughts, words, and deeds in this present life; and which makes every man, in every circle, to a great extent his brother's keeper. But consider Jesus.

His influence was INDIVIDUAL. There was an individuality in His life which acted powerfully upon all whom it reached. But we forget our individuality!

We lose ourselves in the crowd. We follow it, act with it, and thus we forget that, with regard to the religious opinions which we hold, the moral influence which we insensibly exert, the solemn reckoning which we are finally to meet, *"every one of us is to give an account of HIMSELF to God."* "Resolved, that I will live and act as an *individual."* So wrote Harlan Page in his diary; and so he lived and died, and God used his individual influence to the conversion of hundreds. Let us keep in mind the fact, that individual responsibility, duty, and influence, are *untransferable.* We cannot make them over to a church, or to a society, or to another individual. Born as individuals, we live as individuals, and as individuals we die, and shall be judged.

The example of Jesus was HOLY and SANCTIFYING. All who came into His presence could feel how dreadful, yet how attractive, HOLINESS was! Is ours such? Can we in sincerity say, "Follow me, *as I follow Christ?"* Is our example as a religious professor such as to influence others for good?—as a *parent,* such as you would desire your children should imitate?—as a husband or wife, as a brother or sister, as a master or mistress, such as to mold for holiness in this life, and for happiness in the life to come, those whom it daily reaches? Is our example such as to attract them with the beauty of holiness, to impress them with the excellence of Jesus, the service of God, and the solemnity of eternity?

Oh, let your example pencil, like the sun, the image of Christ upon all on whom its transforming rays are reflected. But this can only be *as you yourself follow Christ.* If you would that others be a holy reflection of you, you yourself must be a true and holy reflection of Jesus. Let the light of your influence so shine, that others seeing may rejoice in it. Be a "living epistle of Christ," so legible and lovely as to be known and read of all men, that all may be affected by the reading thereof. Thus men will behold your good works, and glorify your Father which is in heaven.

Consider Jesus—in Filial Subjection *"He was subject unto them."*—Luke 2:51

This was one of the most instructive and lovely traits in our

Lord's character— *His subjection to parental authority.* What period and what condition of life has He not personally impressed with His greatness and hallowed with His sanctity? As Irenaeus beautifully remarks, "He came to save all who are born again unto God; infants and little ones, and children and youths, and those of old age. To little ones He was a little one, sanctifying those of that age, and giving them an example of godliness, righteousness, *and dutiful subjection.*" To this latter feature of our Lord's early life let us direct our present consideration. *"He was SUBJECT unto them."* What a study for the young! what an example for the Christian youth! May the Holy Spirit unfold and impress upon our hearts and lives the holy and beautiful lesson!

The submission of Jesus to His parents was NATURAL. Our Lord was ever true to nature, as nature was ever true to Him, its Creator. Filial submission is an instinct of our being. The existence of parent and child implies the existence of a law prescribing and regulating their relative duties. Had there been no divine precept, and irrespective of all that is positively commanded, nature would prompt the child's duty to its parents. But, what reason dimly teaches, revelation clearly and positively enjoins. When the word of God says,

"This is right," it means, this is just or equitable. Deny the obligation to obey, and you deny the authority to command; ignore the child's duty, and you repudiate the parent's relation. Thus, though our humanity is like a smitten and decayed trunk, the instincts and affections of our nature still cling to it as the ivy clasps with inseparable tenacity the crumbling oak around which it entwines.

The submission of Jesus to His parents was *obediential*—that is, He *obeyed* them. Obedience is the great law of filial piety— disobedience its most unnatural and unholy violation. Under the Mosaic dispensation disobedience to parents was thus fearfully punished: *"If a man has a stubborn and rebellious son who does not obey his father and mother and will not listen to them when they discipline him, his father and mother shall take hold of him and bring him to the elders at the gate of his town. They shall say to the elders, 'This son of ours is stubborn and rebellious. He will not obey us. He is a profligate and a drunkard.' Then all the men of his town shall stone him to death."* (Deut. 21:18-21).

Is the law of the Christian dispensation less binding? Listen to the command— *"Children, OBEY your parents in the Lord, far this is right."*

Again— *"Children, OBEY your parents in all things, for this is well-pleasing unto the Lord."* Beware of this sin! If under the law it was so terribly marked, of how much more severe punishment shall they be counted worthy who violate this law of filial obedience under a dispensation clothed with such solemn sanctions!

Jesus' subjection to His parents was the subjection of LOVE. Filial affection will secure the profoundest reverence for parental authority, and the most implicit obedience to parental command, when that command contravenes no higher law, and asks the surrender of no Christian principle. Oh, how sweet and lovely to submit to the will and obey the command of a parent we deeply reverence and love! It is that invests with such surpassing dignity, holiness, and beauty the unquestioning obedience of a child of God to his Heavenly Father. He obeys God because he loves Him, and there is no obedience so willing, so cheerful, or so complete as the obedience of love. *"If you LOVE me, keep my commandments."* If God has removed your earthly parent, be it your aim to transfer your love, submission, and obedience to your Heavenly Father, *"in whom the fatherless finds mercy."*

Consider Jesus—in Obedience to Divine Law *"He became obedient unto death."*—Phil. 2:8

A higher obedience of Christ is this, than that we have just considered, since it is obedience to a Divine law and to a Heavenly Parent. Those who honor and obey God will not be found willfully and persistently dishonoring and disobeying an earthly one. The higher law, recognized and honored, will mold and regulate all subordinate relations. Oh that the fear of God in our hearts might so shape and sanctify the ties, duties, and trials of this present probationary scene, as to make them subservient to His glory! *"Surely I know that it shall be well with those who fear God."*

But consider the obedience of Jesus. It was SUBSTITUTIONARY obedience. Although consenting to come under a law which He had never broken, no obedience, therefore, to that law was required for Himself. Made under the law as man, He was bound to obey it, but it was the obligation of a Surety. He honored to the utmost every precept, but it was on behalf of those for whom in the covenant of grace He had entered into engagement. It was strictly substitutionary. *"By THE OBEDIENCE of one shall many be made righteous."*

My soul! contemplate this blessed truth. Your covenant Surety Head has answered in your stead all the requirements of the law you had broken, and under whose great condemnation you did lay, thus paying all your great debt and delivering you from a terrible and eternal condemnation.

It was DIVINE obedience. It was the obedience of GOD in our nature, and therefore the righteousness which springs from it is termed the

"Righteousness of God." God, intent upon accomplishing His eternal purpose of saving a portion of the race, provided a divine righteousness for our justification in the obedience of His co-equal and co-eternal Son, and so we are "made the righteousness of God in Him." Glorious truth! *"In your righteousness shall they be exalted."* It *exalts* us above angels, above ourselves, above sin, above condemnation. And because it is divine, it places us before God in the condition of a present and complete justification.

"And lest the shadow of a spot
Should on my soul be found,
He took the robe the Savior wrought,
And cast it all around."

The obedience of Christ is IMPUTED to us by the Spirit. In the same manner by which He became sin for us, we become righteous in Him— *by imputation.* Glorious truth! It is the marrow and fatness of the gospel to those who feel the plague of sin, and who have long starved their souls with the husks and chaff of their own worthless doings. *"Unto whom God imputes righteousness without works."*

It follows that the obedience of Jesus is ours FREELY , because ours by *faith.* Are you, O my soul, bankrupt of all merit and worthiness? Have you *nothing* to pay? Then, listen to the divine declaration—sweeter than angels' chimes— *"By GRACE are you saved through FAITH, and that not of yourselves, it is the gift of God. "*— My soul! It is not yours by your own doings, nor your deservings, nor your sufferings. *"It is by FAITH, that it might be by grace."*

"Lord, I believe! help my unbelief."

Imitate Jesus. Let your walk before the Lord be *obedient.* Let your obedience be loving and unreserved. *"Behold, to OBEY is better than sacrifice, and to HEARKEN than the fat of rams."* Aim, Caleb-like, to 'follow the Lord fully,' standing complete in all the will of God. If Jesus thus fully obeyed for you, all He asks in return is that, if you love Him you will evince that love by OBEYING His commandments. *Love* will make any act of self-sacrifice for Christ sweet, the relinquishment of any sin unhesitating, and the bearing of any cross pleasant.

"Jesus, Your blood and righteousness,
My beauty are, my glorious dress;

Midst flaming worlds, in these arrayed, With joy shall I lift up
my head.

"When from the dust of death I rise,
To take my mansion in the skies,
Even then shall this be all my plea—
Jesus has lived and died for me."

Consider Jesus—in Obedience to Human Law

"Render unto Caesar the things which are Caesar's."—Matt.
22:21

The obedience of Jesus, whether natural or moral—whether
yielded to a divine or a human law—was, like all that He did, worthy of Himself. In no instance did He exhibit anything approaching resistance to constituted authority. Rebellion against Satan
and sin was the only insubordination that marked our Lord's life
on earth. On no occasion did either His doctrine or His practice
come into direct and hostile antagonism with the State. The example before us is striking and conclusive of this. We read that
the "Pharisees took counsel how they might entangle Him in His
talk." They came to Him and inquired, "Is it lawful to give tribute to Caesar, or not?" But Jesus perceived their wickedness, and
said, "Why are you tempting me, you hypocrites?" Had He pronounced it unlawful, caught in their snare, they would instantly
have denounced Him to Herod as teaching treason against Caesar, and thus have evoked the rage of the people and the hostility
of the government. But mark the wisdom and equity with which
He defeated the design and exposed the craft and wickedness of
His enemies, and in so doing, enunciated and enforced the moral
precept which we are now to consider— *"Render unto Caesar the
things that are Caesar's."* The consideration of the duty we owe,
as Christians and citizens, to human law, may not be out of place,
since there exists a strong and growing tendency to override all
human law, and to ignore all civil authority, than which there is
not a more direct violation of God's word or a more palpable violation of the spirit of Christianity.

Jesus recognized the existence of the civil power as an institu-
tion of God himself: *"Everyone must submit himself to the govern-
ing authorities, for there is no authority except that which God has
established. The authorities that exist have been established by
God. Consequently, he who rebels against the authority is rebel-
ling against what God has instituted, and those who do so will
bring judgment on themselves."* (Rom. 13:1, 2). Such must be our
starting-point in all our relations to civil government. Recognizing

the human ordinance to be of divine appointment, the question of reverence to authority and of obedience to law will not reasonably admit of a moment's hesitation.

Jesus rendered unhesitating and implicit submission to both CIVIL and ECCLESIASTICAL law. We have seen it in reference to the State; another example is before us of His reverence for the *Temple*. When "tribute money" was demanded—or the *didachma*, or half-shekel levied for the religious purposes of the temple—He acknowledged its lawfulness, and, lest He should give offence by refusing to obey, He at once wrought a miracle, and paid the money (Matt. 17:24-27). Thus complete was our Lord's obedience to God and man. Upon no civil or religious law would He trample, since He had declared,

"It becomes us to fulfill ALL righteousness." If a law presses upon conscience, or contravenes religious liberty, the remedy is obvious—not disobedience, but repeal; not tumultuous assemblies and inflammatory harangues, but constitutional petition. The Legislature and the Throne are accessible to the lowest and most oppressed subject of the land.

Jesus taught us that subjection to the civil magistrate was not incompatible with reverence to, and the fear of, God. How skillfully He combines them both: *"Render unto Caesar the things that are Caesar's, and unto God the things that are God's."* As disciples of Jesus, as children of God, as Christian citizens, let us so walk as to stand complete in all the divine will. First, and above all, let us obey God. Then will follow, in the Family relation, obedience to parents; in the State, obedience to magistrates; and in the Church of Christ, "obedience to those who have the rule over us" (Heb. 13:17).

"Let Caesar's due be ever paid
To Caesar and his throne;
But consciences and souls were made
To be the Lord's alone."

Consider Jesus—the Object of Popular Favor *When Jesus entered Jerusalem, the whole city was stirred and asked, "Who is this?"* —Matthew 21:10

Jesus was now enthroned upon the highest wave of popular favor. It was, perhaps, the only moment in His earthly history in which it might be said that His popularity was in the ascendant. The sun of human glory now shone upon Him in all its splendor. He was for a moment the idol and the delight of the people. They thronged His path, carpeted it with their garments, strewed it with foliage, and rent the air with their loud and joyous hosannas. All this was strange to Jesus. It was a new page in His history, a new lesson in His life, which would fit Him in all future time to sympathize with and support those who should be subjected to a like perilous ordeal in their Christian career.

We learn that, seasons of earthly prosperity in the experience of the Christian may be perfectly compatible with his close walk with God. The sunshine of God and the smile of the creature may be permitted for a while to blend, tinting with their bright hues the varied forms and objects of existence. These are some of the few 'lights' intermingled with the many 'shadows'—with which God pencils the picture of life. Are our callings prospered, are our homes happy, do friends smile, are neighbors kind, and have the lines fallen to us in pleasant places? These are gleams of light upon our path across the desert, and in them, O my soul! see that you trace a Father's hand, and acknowledge a Father's heart. The picture of your life is not all somber. If the clouds shade, the sunshine brightens it; if judgment frowns, mercy smiles; and if the bread and the water of affliction are at times your appointed portion, with it He gives His love to soothe you, His presence to cheer you, His arm to sustain you, His Heaven to receive you, and says, *"You shall not be forgotten by Me."*

We learn, also, how meekly and lowly a child of God should walk in times of worldly prosperity. Jesus was not inflated with pride, nor lifted up with vainglory by this ebullition of popular favor. Oh, how great the grace required to walk humbly with God in times of worldly prosperity! When

"Jeshurun waxed fat, he kicked." When earthly riches increase, or worldly honors are bestowed, or human applause is lavished, then is the time to flee to the mountain of strength, to the armory of truth, to the solitude of the closet, and to wrestle with God for help to resist and overcome the soul-perils to which all these seductions fearfully expose us. O my soul! be doubly on your guard, be whole nights in your watch-tower, when floating with the tide, wafted by the wind, irradiated with the sunshine of creature good, of earthly prosperity. The world's dizziness, the creature's caresses, the heart's self-satisfaction, would prove your downfall and ruin but for the restraining grace of God.

We also learn *how empty and evanescent a thing is the bubble of popular favor.* When Jesus was come into Jerusalem, "all the city was stirred." But before many days elapsed, the air that rang with His acclaim echoed with His execrations; the voices that then sang "Hosanna!" now shouted "Crucify Him! crucify Him!" and from that very city they led Him out to die. O my soul! bid low for the world's applause; set light by man's favor; be not ensnared by creature smiles. Fill not your censer with the incense, and shape not your sail to catch the breath of, human popularity; still less the favor and adulation of the saints. Their idol today, you may be their object of ridicule tomorrow. 'Hosanna' now, 'Crucify Him' then! Walk humbly with your God. Cling to the faithfulness of the unchanging One, to the friendship of the loving One, to the strength of the Almighty One, and to the compassion and sympathy of the crucified One, and let your Jesus be all in all.

"Earthly friends may fail or leave us,
One day soothe, the next day grieve us,
But this Friend will ne'er deceive us
Oh, how He loves!"

Consider Jesus—the Object of Popular Hate *"He was despised and rejected—a man of sorrows, acquainted with bitterest grief."* Isaiah 53:3

Our Lord's was a chequered history. Lights and shadows thickly blended in the marvelous picture of His life. The lights were but few; the shadows predominated. He did not come into the world to be joyful and happy, but to make others so. Hence the portrait— *"He was despised and rejected—a man of sorrows, acquainted with bitterest grief."* We have just looked upon one of the earthly lights thrown upon the picture; we are now to contemplate one of its dark shadows. From viewing Him as for the moment favored with the adulations of the multitude, we turn to behold Him the object of their bitter scorn and rejection.

"He was despised and rejected—a man of sorrows, acquainted with bitterest grief." There is much in this chapter of Jesus' history worthy of our consideration, and not a little that may be found to reflect in no inconsiderable degree the experience of many Christians. My soul, turn to it. It is a mournful yet a holy picture of Him you love. There is a bitterness in the contemplation, and yet a sweetness indescribably sweet. It is pleasant and cheering to know that your Lord Jesus has gone before you, has trodden the path you tread, and that the sorrow which now rests upon your soul so darkly is but the shadow of the yet darker sorrow that rested upon His.

Jesus was the object of popular hate, because of the DIVINITY OF HIS PERSON. Are real Christians less so? Were we not partakers of the *Divine* nature, we would not drink, in some small degree, of this cup that He drank of. The world despises the image of Christ. If it hated the fair and perfect Original, it will also hate the copy, however dim and imperfect it may be. Be of good cheer, then, if a portion of the world's hatred of Jesus comes upon you. It is a sure evidence that you are in some measure assimilated to your beloved Lord, reflecting His divine and holy image, though marred with many a blot, and shaded with many a cloud.

Jesus was despised because of the UNWORLDLINESS OF HIS LIFE. "The world hates me because I testify of it, that the works thereof are evil." His whole life was one ceaseless testimony against the ungodliness of this ungodly world. It rejected Him because He was holy. In proportion as the life we live is a solemn and consistent protest against the vanities and sinfulness of the world, so will it hate and cast us out. *"You are not of the world; therefore the world hates you."* In His memorable intercessory prayer, Jesus reminds His Father, *"The world has hated them, because they are not of the world, even as I am not of the world."* Accept, then, the world's despisings as your glory. The farther you recede from it, the more powerful your testimony, and the more decided and consistent your unworldly walk, the more virulent will be its malignity, bitter its hate, and wide its separation.

Jesus was equally the object of offence to the world, because of HIS TESTIMONY TO THE TRUTH. On one occasion His enemies took Him to the brow of a hill to hurl Him down to His death, for the testimony which He bore to the Sovereignty of Divine Grace. And it is recorded that, on a similar occasion, many of His disciples went back, and walked no more with Him. The offence of the cross is not ceased. If, through the Holy Spirit's teaching, and the Savior's grace, you are enabled to bear a humble, loving, yet firm and uncompromising testimony to the truth as it is in Jesus, think it not strange if you are called to suffer.

The more spiritual and unadulterated, the more scriptural and unworldly your views of the gospel—its doctrines, its precepts, and its institutions—the more the world, even much of the so-called religious world, will separate from your company, hate, and despise you. But rejoice with exceeding joy if thus counted worthy to suffer shame for Jesus' sake. Keep your eye intently upon Him, and ever remember His animating words—"Be faithful unto death, and I will give you a crown of life." Lord, let the world despise, and even the saints reject me—enough that I am loved and approved of You!

Consider Jesus—as Without Deceit *"He committed no sin, and no deceit was found in his mouth."* —1 Peter 2:22

Purer than the purest crystal, more transparent than the brightest sun, was the character of Jesus. It needed but the visual organ purged from the blinding and distorting effects of sin to have looked into the deepest recesses of His heart, to have seen every pulse, to have read every thought, and to have fathomed every purpose of His soul—so open, transparent, and childlike was He. His foes sought with deception to ensnare Him, but He was too innocent to be ensnared. The moral atmosphere of His being was too pure and translucid for their wicked purposes to find a single fault. They could fix no thought, excite no passion, rouse no imagination within His breast that would have left a taint or a cloud upon that pure, bright spirit of His. What He declared of Satan could with equal truth have been affirmed of ungodly men— *"The prince of this world comes, and has nothing in me."* They found no evil in Him upon which their own sinfulness could work. Wickedness could not for a moment exist in an atmosphere so holy.

Consider the integrity and honesty of Jesus as the *fulfillment of a prophecy:*

"Neither was any deceit in His mouth" (Isa. 53:9). Ponder carefully, my soul, every fulfillment of prophecy concerning your precious Jesus. It will fortify you against the assaults of infidelity and the suggestions of Satan, and enlarge your knowledge of, and deepen your love to, the Savior. Behold the fulfillment of this remarkable prediction—*"Neither was deceit found in His mouth."*

There was no deceit in THE TRUTHS WHICH JESUS TAUGHT. All that the Father revealed to Him He made known to His disciples. He falsified nothing, obscured nothing, kept back nothing. What a lesson for us! Are we ministers of Christ? Then it is our solemn duty to guard against deceit and hypocrisy in our ministrations of the truth. There must be no adulteration of the Word, nothing doubtful in our statement of the Deity and Atonement of Christ, no mental reservation in preaching the doctrines of grace, no denying or neutralizing the Person and work of the Spirit, not the slightest vestige of craftiness or deceitfulness in handling the word of the living God. Woe unto us if we preach not the great truths of the gospel as Christ taught them! We must preach Christ only and wholly, and with Paul be able to testify— *"We have renounced the hidden things of dishonesty, not walking in craftiness, nor handling the word of God deceitfully; but by manifestation of the truth, commending ourselves to every man's conscience in the sight of God."* My soul! beware of holding the truth with guile!

Jesus was guileless in ALL HIS ACTIONS. Everything that He did was as open and as transparent as the light of day. Thus, my soul! learn of Him. Let there be nothing doubtful or ambiguous in your dealings with the world; no deceit or equivocation in your communion with the saints; but let every action and motive and end be as clear and pure as the sun's noontide splendor. Lord, in all things "let integrity and uprightness preserve me."

Above all, Jesus was without guile in HIS WALK BEFORE GOD. He could say, and He only, *"I do always those things which please Him."* It is here, O my soul, you have the most closely to commune with your own heart, and to weigh and ponder and scrutinize every step you take. *"You, Most Upright One, do weigh the path of the just."* Oh, walk before God with a perfect heart, and let your prayer be—Lord, search me! and should I not be real, honest, transparent—graciously, effectually root up every noxious weed, especially that hateful weed of hypocrisy, from Your own garden; and let no principle or motive, aim or end exist but what You approve, and what will be for Your honor and glory. By the sanctifying grace of Your Spirit, by the searching power of Your word, by the hallowed discipline of temptation, affliction, and sorrow, make me *an Israelite indeed, in whom is no deceit!*

Consider Jesus—as Tempted by Satan *"Then was Jesus led up by the Spirit into the wilderness to be tempted by the devil. "*—Matt. 4:1

It is a consolatory reflection to the child of God that, since the temptations of Satan constitute so severe, yet so essential a part of his spiritual training for glory, Jesus, his Surety-Head, was Himself subjected to a like discipline, equally as essential, yet infinitely more severe, to the completeness of His mediatorial character as the High Priest "touched with the feeling of our infirmities." My soul! devoutly consider your Jesus in this interesting point of light, and with faith's lowly hand pluck a rich cluster of refreshing fruit from Him, your living, life-giving, and life-sustaining Vine. Never forget that, through electing love, and most free and sovereign grace, you are an engrafted branch of that Vine; and that all the *fruit* that grows upon, and that all the *fruitfulness* that springs from it (Hos. 14:8), belongs to you. *"He that abides in me, the same brings forth much fruit."*

Of whom was our Jesus tempted? "Of the *devil."* The 'heel' of the 'woman's seed' was now bruised of the 'serpent.' And oh, *what* a bruising! Forty days and forty nights enclosed with the devil in the wilderness, and during that period subjected to every form of fierce assault, until, exhausting his quiver, Satan defeated, retired from the conflict for a season. Such, O my soul! is your great accuser and tempter.

Emancipated from his captivity, you are not yet entirely exempt from his fiery darts. Think it not a strange thing that you should be his target. All the saints of God, more or less, are subjected to a like discipline. He incited David to number the people, smote job with great boils, sifted Peter as wheat, hindered Paul again and again; and, selecting the most shining mark of all, hurled his darts, thick and flaming, at the Lord Himself. Cheer up, then! your great adversary is wounded, deadly wounded; you have to do with a conquered foe, ever under the control of the "Lion of the tribe of Judah," and you yourself shall bruise Satan under your feet shortly.

And what were some of the darts hurled by Satan at Jesus? The devil tempted Him to distrust God, to commit self-destruction, to yield to the splendor, riches, and possessions of the world, to pay him religious homage. Such was the fiery ordeal through which the Son of God passed. And such are some of the darts by which the devil seeks to wound your conscience and disturb your peace. In need, you are tempted to distrust God; in despondency, to self- violence; in ambition, to grasp the world; and in the idolatrous propensities of your nature, to love and worship the creature more than the Creator. O my soul! count it a great honor to be tempted by the same tempter and with the same temptations as your blessed Jesus, through whom you shall get the victory.

Jesus was now being made like unto His brethren. It was necessary, in order to His perfect sympathy with us, that He should be in all points tempted like as we are, yet without sin (Heb. 4:15). Fly to Him, then, O tempted one! He is not a High Priest who can be indifferent to your present assault, since He was pierced by Satan, and in a measure is still pierced by the fiery darts which now pierce you. *Accept your present temptation as sent to make you better acquainted with His preciousness, His sympathy, His grace, His changeless love.*

Regard it, also, as a part of that spiritual discipline that is to teach your hands to war, and your fingers to fight in the present with the world, the flesh, and the devil; and to prepare you to take your place among the palm-bearing conquerors of heaven, who overcame him by the blood of the Lamb, who shout the victor's song, and cast their crowns at Jesus' feet. "Take the shield of faith, with which you shall be able to quench all the fiery darts of the wicked."

Consider Jesus—as Afflicted *"He was afflicted."*—Isa. 53:7

For this Jesus was born. His mission to our world involved it. In the righteous arrangement of God, sin and suffering, even as holiness and happiness, are one and inseparable. He came to destroy the works of the devil; and sin, being Satan's master-work, Jesus could only destroy it as He Himself suffered, just as He could only 'abolish death' as He Himself died. He was truly "a man of sorrows, and acquainted with grief." In the gospel according to Isaiah—the fifty-third chapter of which might have been written by a historian recording the event of the Savior's sufferings *after* it had transpired, rather than by a prophet predicting it seven hundred years before it took place—the circumstances of our Lord's afflictive life are portrayed with a fidelity of narration and vividness of description which can only find their explanation in *"the Spirit of Christ, which was in him, testifying beforehand of the sufferings of Christ and the glory that should follow."*

"He was afflicted." What touching and expressive words are these! Consider them carefully, my soul. Attempt, if it be possible, an analysis of your Lord's afflictions. And the first feature that presents itself is, that He was afflicted BY GOD. How clearly is this fact put— *"We did esteem Him smitten by God and afflicted. It pleased the Lord to bruise Him. He has put Him to grief."* Was Jesus, then, afflicted of God? So are we! The God that smote Him, smites us; the paternal hand that mingled His cup, prepares ours. O my soul! refer all your trials to God. Be not tossed about amid the troubled waves of *second causes,* but trace all your afflictions, however dark, bitter, and painful, directly to the wisdom, righteousness, and love of your Father in heaven.

"Himself has done it." Enough, Lord, if I but see Your hand and Your heart guiding, shaping, and controlling the whole.

Jesus was afflicted BY MAN. "He was despised and rejected *by men."* Beloved, how many of our trials, and how much of our wounding, springs from the same source! This should teach us to cease from man, and to put no confidence in the arm of flesh, since ofttimes the staff we thought so pleasant, and on which we leaned so confidingly, is the first to pierce the hand that too fondly and too closely pressed it.

Jesus was afflicted IN THE SOUL. "My soul is sorrowful, even unto death." Is not *soul*-sorrow our greatest, even as the soul is the most spiritual, precious, and immortal part of our nature? Is your soul-sorrowful? Are you conflicting with sin, harassed by doubts, depressed with fears, sorrowful almost unto death?—

consider Jesus as having passed through a like soul-discipline, and uplift your prayer to Him—"My heart is overwhelmed; lead me to the Rock that is higher than I."

Jesus was BODILY afflicted . We do not read of actual disease of body, but we do read of bodily suffering such as infinitely surpasses all to which we can possibly be subjected; and endured, be it remembered, O my soul! for YOU!

This may be the Lord's affliction in your case. A diseased body, distressing nervousness, extreme debility your daily cross. Be it so—it is all the fruit of everlasting and eternal love. Receive it believingly, endure it patiently, and be anxious only that the rod thus laid upon you by a Father's hand should bloom and blossom with holy fruit to the glory of God.

Affliction was a SCHOOL for Jesus. *"He LEARNED obedience by the things which He suffered."* Not less is it ours. We enter it, for the most part, with but a mere notional, theoretical acquaintance with God, and with Christ, and with our own selves; but sorrow's hallowed discipline transforms us into *experimental* Christians, and, gazing upon the lowly Savior, we exclaim—"I have heard of You by the hearing of the ear; but now my eye sees You. Therefore I abhor myself, and repent in dust and ashes." O my soul! if this be the result of affliction, let the scythe mow you, the furnace dissolve you, the flail thrash you, the sieve sift you; it will but conform you the more closely to your once afflicted, suffering Lord.

Consider Jesus—Our Paymaster *"He was oppressed. "*—Isa. 53:7

The Hebrew word here rendered "oppressed," signifies to *exact,* or, to demand payment. It is so rendered in the following passage— *"The creditor shall not EXACT of his neighbor, nor of his brother, in the year of release."* The word *taskmaster* comes from the same root; and as there is no noun prefixed to the original, the words may be fitly rendered—it was *exacted* of Him, *demanded, required,* and He was 'afflicted,' or, He *answered.* A truer view of the office and work of the Lord Jesus does not exist; nor is there a more gracious and comforting point of light in which a poor, sin-burdened, guilt- oppressed soul can study Him.

By nature all are God's debtors, owing Him supreme love, perfect holiness, entire obedience, and unreserved service—yes, our whole being, body, soul, and spirit. To meet this great debt, we are—by nature, in consequence of the fall, morally and utterly unable—bankrupt of all righteousness and strength, having "nothing to pay." No will, no heart, no might—in a word, there being in us no good thing. O my soul! ponder this your state by nature—owing an infinite debt to God, with no possible way of discharging a single fraction of the claim, deserving to be cast into the prison of eternal punishment until you have paid the uttermost farthing.

But consider Jesus as the Church's great PAYMASTER and SURETY. Jesus, in eternity, entered into a bond, signed with His own hand, and afterwards sealed with His own blood, to free us from all this great debt. In fulfillment of that covenant engagement, in the fullness of time He was born of a woman, made under the law, and by His perfect obedience and atoning death, He gave full satisfaction to the Divine government, and so Law and Justice exacted from Him the obligation He had undertaken to meet. And now was fulfilled His own prophecy concerning Himself— *"Then I restored that which I took not away."* Jesus restored the glory of God, of which He had not robbed Him. He satisfied Divine justice, which He had never injured. He fulfilled a Law He had never broken, and so restored to it a righteousness He had never taken away. And He made satisfaction for sins He had never committed; and so, *"He restored that which He took not away."*

Sin is a debt—Jesus paid it when He bore our sins in His own body on the tree. *Obedience* is a debt—Jesus paid it when, by the obedience of One, many were made righteous. *Death* is a debt—Jesus paid it when He bowed His head on the cross and gave up the spirit. And when thus we behold Him dragged into the court of human justice, and sentenced to a felon's death—and when we follow Him to the garden of His sorrow, sweating great drops of blood, and thence to Calvary, and see Him nailed to the accursed tree—suffering, bleeding, dying—what do we behold but the *exacting* from Him the full payment of the bond for the honoring of which He had entered into an eternal suretyship on His people's behalf?

What life and liberty are bound up in these words—*"I forgave you all that great debt!"* Believing soul, the debtor's prison is no longer your abode. The bond is cancelled, and God, the Creditor, fully satisfied with the Atonement of His beloved Son, has given a full discharge both to Him and to us, in that He raised Him from the dead. No longer, then, look at your sins, unworthiness, nothingness, and poverty; but look to Jesus, and, looking constantly by faith at Him, walk in the holy, happy liberty of one all whose debt is cancelled, and for whom there is now no condemnation. Is Jesus your Paymaster, O my soul?

Then He has equally engaged to provide for your *temporal* needs, to deliver you out of all your difficulties, and to enable you to meet all your worldly engagements. Surely He who has paid your greater debt to God, will help you honorably to pay your lesser debt to man.

Consider Jesus—as Forsaken by Man *"Then all the disciples forsook Him, and fled."*—Matt. 26:56

What a sad contrast does this picture present to the one we have just been viewing— *"Jesus, our fellow-sufferer."* His time of suffering has now come, but, lo! "all His disciples have forsaken Him, and fled." Is there nothing, my soul, in this affecting and significant fact from which you may gather much that is instructive and consolatory concerning your own condition? We have been contemplating the sympathy of Jesus with His afflicted saints. And oh, what heart can conceive, or imagery portray, the reality, humanity, and tenderness of that sympathy! In all our afflictions He is afflicted, in all our trials He is tried, in all our persecutions He is persecuted, in all our temptations He is tempted. My soul! there is no sympathy among men, saints, or angels, that can compare with Christ's. And yet how thankful should you be for the smallest measure of human sympathy given you. It may have been, and doubtless was, but as a drop in comparison of the ocean-fullness of Christ's; nevertheless, that drop has proved inexpressibly and immeasurably soothing, sweetening many a bitter trial, gilding many a cloud, and lighting the pressure of many a burden. For this uplift your praiseful heart to God.

But even this drop of 'creature sympathy' afforded you was denied your suffering Lord. How earnestly and touchingly did He ask it! *"Stay here and watch with me, while I go yonder and pray."* And when from the scene of His conflict and anguish He returned, sobbing and gory, to bury His grief in their compassion and love—lo! He found them sleeping! How gentle, yet how searching, His rebuke— *"Could you not watch with me one hour?"* What condition in the experience of the saints does this page of our Lord's history meet? It meets a sad and painful one—one which could only thus be met—the lack of human sympathy.

You are, perhaps, in a condition which needs the sympathy of a kind and loving spirit, and your sad and clinging heart yearns for it. But, as in the case of your sorrowing Lord, it slumbers at the moment that you most needed its wakeful, watchful expression. And yet its very absence may prove your richest soothing, by bringing you into a closer experience of the sympathy of Jesus. Having Himself felt its need and its lack, He is all the more fitted, as your fellow-sufferer, to sympathize with, and supply your present need.

You are, perhaps, suffering from MISPLACED AND WOUNDED AFFECTION. You have naturally allowed the fibers of your heart to entwine around some object of its warm and clinging love; but chilled affection, or the whisper of envy, or the venomed tooth of slander, has wrenched those fibers from their stem, and trailed them, torn and bleeding, in the dust. How like Jesus now you are, of whose loved disciples it is recorded, *"They all forsook Him, and fled."*

Or, you are suffering from BETRAYED AND DISAPPOINTED CONFIDENCE. One you thought a friend, tender and true, has deserted you; a judgment upon whose guidance you leaned has misled you; a source upon whose supplies you depended has failed you; a confidence in which you too implicitly reposed has betrayed you; and thus you are learning the lesson Jesus learned when, *"all His disciples forsook Him, and fled."*

Cheer up, my soul! there is One who has promised never to leave you. When father and mother, husband and wife, lover and friend, forsake you, the Lord will take you up. He who was deserted by friends and followers, will cling to you in prosperity and in adversity, in weal and in woe, with unfaltering fidelity and unchanging love; and though all forsake you, yet will He not in life, in death, and through eternity. How great and precious the divine promise—"They may forget, yet I will not." "Jesus Christ, the same yesterday, today, and forever." Precious Jesus! though all forsake me, as all forsook You; yet YOU will never leave me, nor forsake me!

Consider Jesus—as Forsaken by God *"My God, my God, why have You forsaken me?"*—Matt. 27:46

My soul! was it not enough that your Lord should be forsaken of *man* in His sorrow? Was it essential to the accomplishment of your salvation, and to your support and comfort in seasons of soul desertion and darkness, that He should likewise be forsaken of *God?* Yes! it *must* be so. The history of the universe never presented such an abandonment—a being so holy, and yet so entirely and so severely forsaken of God and man—as that which Jesus was now experiencing upon the accursed tree. With what a depth of emphasis that word must have sounded from His pale lips, quivering with agony— *"'My God, my God, why have YOU FORSAKEN me?'* You, my Father—You whose glory I am vindicating, whose government I am honoring, whose Name I am glorifying, whose Church I am redeeming—why, my God, my God, have YOU forsaken me? I can endure to be abandoned by man, but to be forsaken by YOU, my Father, in the hour of my deepest sorrow, at the moment of my keenest suffering, is the bitterest ingredient in my cup of bitter, the darkest hue in my cloud of darkness." Let us devoutly consider Jesus as passing through this eclipse of His soul, and receive the holy instruction and comfort the spectacle was designed to convey.

Of WHOM was Jesus forsaken? *His Father.* And when, O my soul! you walk in a sense of divine desertion, who is it that says to you, *"For a small moment have I forsaken you, but with great mercies will I gather you?"* —it is your *Father* in heaven. It is a *Father's* momentary withdrawment; and although this thought adds keenness to the discipline and intensity to the cloud, is there no consolation in knowing that the hiding is paternal—a Father secreting Himself from His child—and but for a moment? Thus, though He hides

Himself, He is a *Father* still.

But, what was a cloud of thick, all-enshrouding darkness to Jesus is salvation's light to us. Even as His sorrow is our joy, His wounds our healing, His death our life—so His abandonment on the cross, as a foreign divine expresses it, is "our bridge to heaven; an unfathomable abyss for all our sins, cares, and anxieties; the charter of our citizenship, the key whereby we may open the secret chamber of communion with God."

Thus, if you are, O my soul! walking in darkness and have no light, let the thought be as a ray playing on the brow of your cloud, that, it is not the darkness of hell and condemnation, but the darkness only through which all the 'children of light' more or less travel—the darkness with which the Sun of Righteousness Himself was enshrouded—and which, when it is past, will make the sunshine of God's love and the Savior's presence all the sweeter, dearer, brighter.

And how did Jesus deport Himself in this season of Divine forsaking? What supported and comforted Him during this total and dreadful eclipse through which His sinless soul passed? *He trusted in God.* His *faith* could still exclaim,

"MY God, MY God." So lean upon your covenant God, O you children of light walking in darkness. As the veiling clouds, though they hide, cannot extinguish the sun, neither can your gloomy seasons of Divine desertion extinguish one beam of the Savior's love to you. If all is dark—a hidden God, an absent Savior, a frowning providence—now is the time *to have faith in God.*

"Who is among you *that walks in darkness, and has no light?*

let him trust in the name of the lord, and stay upon his God." Stay yourself upon His covenant faithfulness and unchanging love, and believe that Jesus intercedes for you in heaven, and that soon you shall reach that blissful world where your sun shall no more go down, nor your moon withdraw itself.

"Through waves, and clouds, and storms,
He gently clears your way:
O Wait His time—your darkest night
Shall end in brightest day."
Consider Jesus—in Loneliness
"And shall leave me alone."—John 16:32

Jesus, for the most part, lived a lonely and solitary life. It was of necessity so. There was much in His mission, more in His character, still more in His person, that would baffle the comprehension, and estrange from Him the interest and the sympathy of the world; compelling Him to retire within the profound solitude of His own wondrous Being.

The TWOFOLD NATURE of Jesus contributed essentially to the loneliness of His life. The 'great mystery of godliness, God manifest in the flesh,' would of itself confine Him to an orbit of being infinitely remote from all others. Few could sympathize with His perfect sinlessness as man, fewer still with His essential dignity as God.

As it was with the Lord, so, in a measure, is it with the disciple. The spiritual life of the renewed man is a profound mystery to the unregenerate. Strangers experimentally to the New Birth, they cannot understand the 'divine nature' of which all believers are 'partakers.' Nor this only. Even among the *saints* we shall often find our path a lonely and solitary one. How much may there be in—the truths which we hold, in the church to which we belong, and even in the more advanced stages of Christian experience we have traveled, which separates us in fellowship and sympathy from many of the Lord's people. Alas! that it should be so.

Our Lord's WORK contributed much to His sense of loneliness. How expressive His words—"I have food to eat *that you know not of.* My food is to do the will of Him who sent me, and to finish His work." And so may it be with us. The Christian work confided to us by Jesus may be of such a character, and in such a sphere, as very much to isolate us from the sympathy and aid of the saints. It has concealed temptations, hidden trials, unseen difficulties, distasteful employments, with which we can expect but little sympathy and pity; compelling us, like our blessed Lord, to eat our 'food' in solitude. But, oh, sweet thought! the Master whom you serve knows your appointed sphere of labor, and will, by His succouring grace, soothing love, and approving smile, share and bless your lonely meal.

The TEMPTATION of Jesus rendered His path lonely. He was alone with the devil forty days and nights in the wilderness. No bosom friend, no faithful disciple, was there to speak a word of soothing sympathy. And are not our temptations solitary? How few are cognizant of, or even suspect, the fiery assaults through which we, perhaps, are passing. Of the skeptical doubts, the blasphemous suggestions, the vain thoughts, the unholy imaginations transpiring within our inner man they know nothing—and this intensifies our sense of loneliness. But the Tempted One knows it all, and will not leave us to conflict single-handed with the tempter, but will with the temptation make a way for our escape. "The Lord knows how to deliver the godly out of temptation."

The SOUL-SORROW of Jesus rendered His path lonely. Prophesying of

Himself, He said, "I have trodden the winepress *alone; and of the people there was none with me.*" How lonely may be your grief, O believer! None share your sorrow, few understand it. You are 'as a sparrow alone on the house- top.' There are none to watch with you in the garden of your anguish—your wounded heart, like the stricken deer, bleeds and mourns in secret. But your sorrow is all known to your loving, compassionate Savior; whose wisdom appointed it, whose love sent it, whose grace sustains it, and who will soothe and strengthen you with His tenderest sympathy. Let your labor of love, your lonely sorrow, throw you more entirely upon, and bring you into closer, more believing, and more loving relations with, the Savior; wean you more from the creature; separate you more from the world; and set you more supremely apart for God. Oh! then you will thank Him for the discipline of *loneliness* as among the holiest and most precious blessings of your life!

Consider Jesus—as Not Alone *"And yet I am not alone, because the Father is with me."*—John 16:32

There is a sweetness in every cup, a light in every cloud, a presence in every solitude of the Christian's experience. It was so with Jesus, who will mold all His followers like unto Himself. We have just considered Him in *loneliness*—forsaken by man, deserted by God. But now comes the alleviation—the sweetening of the bitter, the gilding of the cloud, the soothing of the solitude. He was never less alone than at the moment that He mournfully said to His retiring disciples, *"You shall leave me alone;"* for, as if immediately recovering Himself from the painful sense of MAN'S DESERTION, He added,

"And yet I am not alone, because the Father is with Me." No; Jesus never was really alone. Shunning human society, and plunging into solitude the most profound, as He often did, His Father's presence was there to sweeten and soothe it, to replenish and strengthen Him for the work He had given Him to do, and to make those long midnight hours of holy watching and wrestling prayer, melodious with the music, and radiant with the sunshine of heaven. Oh yes, Jesus was *not* all alone!

Nor are you really alone, O child of God! Alone, indeed, you may be as to human companionship, affection, and, sympathy. Nor is this trial of your spirit to be lightly spoken of. God has, perhaps, given you by nature a confiding, warm, and clinging heart; a heart that yearns for companionship, that seeks a loving, sympathizing friend, to whose bosom you may confide the thoughts and emotions of your own—"another self, a kindred spirit, with whom you may lessen your cares by sympathy, and multiply your pleasures by participation." But the blessing is not permitted you; or, if once possessed and enjoyed, is possessed and enjoyed no longer—the coldness of death, the yet colder and more painful chill of 'alienated affection and changed friendship', has left your heart like a tree of autumn, stripped of its foliage, through whose leafless branches the wintry blast moans piteously.

But this discipline of the affections, though intensely painful to a heart gushing with sensibility like yours, may prove one of the costliest blessings to the soul. A heart that is satiated with the creature, has little or no place or yearning, for Christ. And when the Lord is resolved to be supreme, and finds a 'rival sovereign' enthroned, or a 'created idol' enshrined, He wisely and lovingly removes it, to make room for Himself. Oh, it is when the heart is withered like grass—when its chords are all broken, and its fibers are all torn, and silence, desolation, and solitude reign within—wounded by one, betrayed by another, forsaken by all— that Jesus approaches and occupies the vacant place, takes down the harp from the willow, repairs and retunes it, then breathing His own sweet Spirit upon its wires, wakes it, to the richest harmonies of praise, thanksgiving, and love. My Father, I cannot be alone, blessed with Your presence, solaced with Your love, cheered with Your fellowship, kept by Your power, and wisely, gently led through the solitude of the wilderness, home to be with Yourself forever! "You are near, O Lord!"

"You are near—yes, Lord, I feel it—
You are near wherever I rove;
And though sense would try conceal it,
Faith often whispers it to love.

"Am I fearful? You will take me
Underneath Your wings, my God!
Am I faithless? You will make me
Bow beneath Your chastening rod.

"Am I drooping? You are near me,
Near to bear me on my way;
Am I pleading? You will hear me—Hear and answer when I pray.

"Then, O my soul, since God does love you,
Faint not, droop not, do not fear;
For, though His heaven is high above you,
He Himself is ever near."

Consider Jesus—in Soul-trouble
"Now My soul is deeply troubled." —John 12:27

In this lay our Lord's greatest suffering—His *soul-sorrow.* Compared with this, the lingering, excruciating tortures of the cross—the extended limbs, the quivering nerves, the bleeding wounds, the burning thirst—were, as nothing. This was physical, the other spiritual; the one, the suffering of the body, the other, the anguish of the soul. Let a vessel traversing the ocean keep afloat, and she may still plough the deep and brave the tempest; but let the proud waves burst in upon her and she sinks. So long as our blessed Lord endured outwardly the gibes and insults and calumnies of men, not a complaint escaped His lips; but, when the wrath of God, endured as the Surety-Head of His people, entered within His holy soul, then the wail of agony rose strong and piercing—"Save Me, O God, for the floodwaters are up to My neck. Deeper and deeper I sink into the mire; I can't find a foothold to stand on. I am in deep water, and the floods overwhelm Me. I am exhausted from crying for help; My throat is parched and dry. My eyes are swollen with weeping, waiting for my God to help Me." Psalm 69:1-3

How true is God's word—"The spirit of a man will sustain his infirmity; *but a wounded spirit, who can bear?*" Such was Christ's. And why was His soul troubled? One rational answer alone can be given—He was now bearing sin and, consequently, the punishment of sin—the wrath of God overwhelming His soul. This was the 'cup' which He prayed might, 'if possible, pass from Him.' Divine justice, finding the sins of God's elect meeting on His holy soul, exacted full satisfaction and inflicted the utmost penalty. And thus a glorious gospel truth shines out of this terrible cloud of Jesus' soul-sorrow—that is, the *substitutionary character* and the *atoning nature* of His sufferings and death. Upon no reasonable ground other than this can we satisfactorily account for His language— *"My soul is exceeding sorrowful, even unto death."* But turn we now from Jesus to His saints.

Believer in Jesus, yours is, perhaps, *soul-sorrow*. A sense of sin troubles you, the consciousness of guilt distresses you, and you begin to think you know nothing of God's pardoning love. Oh, what would you not give to be *quite sure* that your sins were all forgiven for Jesus' sake!

Or, your soul is in sorrow, perhaps, from the painful loss of the evidences of your saintship and adoption. Like Bunyan's pilgrim, you have dropped the 'white stone with the new name,' and, retracing your steps, mournful and sad, to recover it, you exclaim, *"Oh that it were with me as in days that are past, when the candle of the Lord shone round about me."*

Or, you are, perhaps, in soul-distress in consequence of the corroding doubts and distressing fears which assail you; and instead of going on your heavenly way rejoicing, forgetting the things that are behind, and pressing on towards those things that are before, your time is spent, as just intimated, in searching for Christian evidences, and in battling with unbelieving doubts and fears.

Or, perhaps, your soul may be in sorrow because you discern so little love to God, so faint a resemblance to the Savior, and so little real, vital, operative religion in your life—in a word, the spiritual life beating with a pulse so sickly and faint, that your soul is cast down within you.

One word of encouragement. Be thankful to God for this soul-sorrow—it is *a sure evidence of spiritual life*. A soul dead in sin is insensible to any real distress because of sin; a heart destitute of love to God, feels no distress because it does not love Him. A graceless sinner never longs for grace: an unrenewed person never thirsts for holiness, and a dead soul never breathes after life. Take heart, then, O believer, for your soul-sorrow is the prelude to your soul's eternal joy.

But see to it that Christ has alone to do with your present sorrow. Take it only to Him. It will prove the greatest, the holiest joy of your life, if it makes you better acquainted with Jesus. O sweet and welcome sorrow, which He who changed the water into wine changes into a joy unspeakable and full of glory. Any sorrow, Lord, if it but enthrone YOU more supremely upon my heart, to reign—"the Lord of every motion there."

Consider Jesus—in Communion with God

"And in the morning, rising up a great while before day, He went out, and departed into a solitary place, and there prayed." —Mark 1:35

To whom can this impressive picture of high devotion properly apply but to Him whose life was one continuous act of prayer; whose vital and all- pervading atmosphere was communion with God? Jesus literally "walked with God." As man, He was deeply conscious of the spiritual necessities of man; and as the God-man Mediator, He felt the need of looking up to the Strong One for strength, to the Wise One for wisdom, to the Loving One for sympathy—in a word, to His Father in Heaven for the constant replenishing of His daily need from the boundless resources of His own Infinite Being, for the great work His Father had given Him to do.

Wise will it be for us to consider Jesus touching the article of *prayer*. If He, the sinless One, He the mighty One, He the divine One felt, deeply and momentarily felt, the need of drawing from above by the breath of prayer those supplies needful for the accomplishment of His work and for the glorifying of His Father, oh, how much more have we need that prayer should precede, accompany, and follow every step we take; that communion with God should prompt, aid, and sanctify every act of our lives; that, in a word, in imitation of our blessed Lord, we should often rise up a great while before day, and depart into a solitary place, and, before secular and worldly things took possession of our minds, *give ourselves to prayer.*

My soul! consider this precious privilege! Is there a holier, sweeter, or more needful one? Consider Jesus in this matter, and form your prayerful life upon the model of His. He always approached God in prayer as His Father. His spirit, His language, His approach was *filial*. "Holy Father." "My Father." Equally is this your privilege. God stands to you in the close, the endeared relation of a *Father* by adopting grace, and it were a dishonor done to His name, and an ignoring of His Fatherhood, to approach Him in prayer in any other relation and character than this. Oh, feel that, when you pour out your sinful heart, your sorrowful heart, your broken heart before Him, you are pouring it all into a *Father's* ear, a *Father's* bosom.

The prayer of Jesus was REAL COMMUNION with God. So let yours be, O my soul! Rest not content with the form of prayer, the duty of prayer, the act of prayer. Be not satisfied unless conscious of the listening ear of God, the responding heart of Jesus, the vital breathing of the Spirit. Oh, let your communion with heaven be a blessed *reality*. Do not leave the Mercy-Seat without some evidence that you have been in solemn, holy, precious audience with the Invisible One. It may be the evidence of contrition, of humiliation, of confession; or, of simple faith, of child-like love, of filial trust—but leave it not until God in Christ has spoken to you face to face. Oh, whatever your sin, or sorrow, or need may be, rise amid the twilight shadows which drape your soul, and give yourself to prayer!

By this example of Jesus, we are taught the necessity and the blessedness of secret prayer. "He departed into a *solitary place,* and there prayed." My soul! enter into your closet, and shut the door behind you, and pray to your Father in secret. You have secret declensions to confess, secret sorrows to unveil, secret wants to present, secret blessings to crave. Away, then, to your chamber. Take with you the blood of Jesus, and with your hand of faith upon His Word, *open all your heart* in filial, loving confidence, to God, and, in paternal love, He will open all the treasures of His heart to you. Let nothing keep you from secret communion with God. Business, family, friends must all give place to this, if you want soul prosperity. Five minutes alone with Jesus will carry you through five hours of toil and trial. "Come, my people, enter into your chamber." Lord! I come!

Consider Jesus—in the Forgiveness of Injury *"Father, forgive them; for they know not what they do."*—Luke 23:34

If the Christian precept of FORGIVENESS be estimated by the magnitude of the injury forgiven, then these words of Jesus present to our view a forgiveness of an inconceivable and unparalleled injury. *The greatest crime man ever committed* was the crucifixion of the Son of God; and yet, for the *forgiveness* of that crime, the Savior prays at the very moment of its perpetration, fully persuaded of the sovereign efficacy of the blood His enemies were now shedding, to blot out the enormous guilt of the sin of shedding it.

This interceding prayer of Jesus for His murderers was in the sweetest harmony with all He had previously taught. On no gospel precept did He seem to lay greater stress than the precept of forgiveness of injury. *"FORGIVE, and you shall be forgiven." "When you stand praying, FORGIVE, if you have anything against any."*

"But if you do not FORGIVE, neither will your Father who is in heaven forgive you your trespasses." "How often shall my brother sin against me, and I FORGIVE him? Until seven times? Jesus says unto him, I say not unto you, Until seven times, but UNTIL SEVENTY TIMES SEVEN."

Where shall we find any Christian precept enjoined in our Lord's teaching so lucidly explained, so frequently enforced, or so impressively illustrated, as *the forgiveness of injury?*

Thus, what Jesus taught in His preaching, He embodied in His example. In addition to this prayer for His murderers, uttered amid the insults and tortures they were at that moment inflicting—see Him healing the ear of one of the band sent to arrest Him; see Him turning a look of forgiving love upon the penitent dying at His side; listen to the charge He gave to His apostles after His resurrection, to 'begin' their work of unfolding the message of salvation 'at Jerusalem,' whose inhabitants were to be the first to drink of the Rock they had smitten, and the first to wash in the blood they had shed. Oh, was ever forgiveness of injury like Christ's? My soul, sit down at His feet, yes, beneath His cross, and learn the lesson now so solemnly taught, and so touchingly enforced, even the lesson of forgiving and praying for your enemies, and for all who despitefully use you— *"Father, forgive them!"*

We cannot pass through an ungodly world, nor even mingle with the saints, and not be often unjustly misrepresented, strangely misunderstood, and unkindly wounded. The lily grows among thorns; the lamb goes forth among wolves. So Jesus reminded His disciples. And yet it is the saddest thought of all that, our deepest wounds are those which we receive in the house of our friends. There are no injuries so unexpectedly inflicted, or so keenly felt, as those which we receive from our fellow-saints.

But, oh, the blessedness of writing as Christ did, those injuries upon the sands, which the next flood-tide of forgiving love shall instantly and utterly efface!

Standing before this marvelous spectacle of forgiveness—Christ on the cross praying for His slayers—what true believer in Jesus can think of the wrong done to himself, the injustice inflicted, the pain produced, and yet harbor in his heart a revengeful, unforgiving spirit? My soul, go to the brother who has offended, to the sister who has wounded you, and say, "In lowly imitation of my Savior, I FORGIVE you all that wrong." "Therefore, as God's chosen people, holy and dearly loved, clothe yourselves with compassion, kindness, humility, gentleness and patience. Bear with each other and forgive whatever grievances you may have against one another. Forgive as the Lord forgave you." Col. 3:12-13

This prayer of Jesus was ANSWERED. On the Day of Pentecost among the three thousand converts were many of His murderers, who, pierced in their heart, washed in the fountain their own hands had opened, and were forgiven. So soon did God answer the prayer of His Son! Let us, like Jesus, "pray for those who despitefully use us." Who can tell how soon God may answer, turn their hearts, convert and save them?

Consider Jesus—in the Exercise of Praise *"I will declare your name to my brothers; in the presence of the congregation I will sing your praises."* —Hebrews 2:12

These are the words of Jesus quoted by the apostle from a prophetical psalm concerning Him. We have considered Him as teaching us by His example to *pray;* it may promote our personal holiness by considering Him as teaching us to PRAISE. Praise is an element of the gospel. It entered essentially, if not prominently, into our Lord's personal life. "A man of sorrow," though He was— oftener seen to weep than to smile—yet there were moments when gleams of joy shone upon His soul, and strains of praise breathed from His lips.

Our Lord was of a THANKFUL spirit, and a *thankful* spirit is a *praiseful* spirit. How often the words were on His lips, "I *thank* You, O Father." He thanked God for the sovereignty of His grace for manifesting Himself to His disciples, for the food He was about to distribute, and over the grave of the friend He was about to raise from the dead. In all things Jesus was of a *thankful,* and therefore of a *praiseful* spirit.

And so, my soul, should *you* be! You have everything to praise God for. For the GLORIOUS GOSPEL of the blessed God; which, in the blessed announcements it makes of full pardon, of free justification, of gracious adoption, of present grace and future glory—is praise, all praise, eternal praise. There is not one announcement in the gospel to dishearten or repel a poor, penitent sinner. To such it is a 'joyful sound' without one jarring note, a salvation without a condition, a righteousness without a work, a pardon without money, a heaven without human merit or purchase—all the *free gift of God's most free and unmerited grace.* Is not *this* sufficient to awaken the deepest gratitude and the loudest praise in your soul?

And, O my soul! what shall be said of the praise due from you for the GIFT OF JESUS? Can you think of Him for a moment, and not feel your whole soul thrilling with thanksgiving and tremulous with praise? Oh, praise God for Jesus—for such a divine yet such a human Savior—for such a life, for such a death, for such a righteousness, and for such an Atonement as His. Is there no deep response of your heart to the thankful, praiseful words of the apostle—

"Thanks be unto God, for His unspeakable gift?" Oh, praise Him for such a lovely and loving, for such a gracious and precious Savior, but for whom, you had been lost forever!

And have you not reason to praise God for YOUR CONVERSION? Oh, what a wonder of sovereign grace that ever you were brought out of nature's darkness into God's marvelous light! That, ever divine power drew you, and divine love chose you, and divine blood cleansed you, and a divine righteousness was imputed to you! That, ever you did hear the voice of Jesus, when lying in your blood, cast out to the loathing of yourself, saying to you,

"Live!" And that then He washed you, and clothed you, and decked you with ornaments, and put a fair chain on your neck, a crown and a mitre on your head, and you became lovely through His loveliness put upon you—a *king* and a *priest* unto God! Praise, oh, praise Him loudly for that happy day when, having betrothed you in eternity, He savingly drew you to Himself, and you became His. Can you recall the memory of that blissful hour, and not make the desert ring with your loudest, sweetest praise?

"Oh! to grace, how great a debtor!"

My soul! seek from God the spirit of thankfulness, and cultivate habitually the grace of praise. It is a soul-purifying and a God-glorifying grace. It keeps the heart in perpetual bloom, and *converts the life into a daily psalm!* Praise God for all—praise Him for the blessings—of His *providence,* for the barrel of meal and for the cruse of oil that have not failed, for the providence that brightens, for the sorrow that shades, for the mercy that smiles, and for the judgment that frowns—for God's *love* breathing through all. Thus shall you be learning to sing the 'new song,' and to unite in the never ending music of heaven, where—

"Praise shall employ our noblest powers,

While immortality endures."

Consider Jesus—in the Avoidance of Offence

"Lest we should offend. "—Matt. 17:27

How truly was our Lord Jesus 'harmless' because He was 'undefiled.' In Him was no sin. That His Gospel should have been an offence to the scribes and Pharisees, and that His cross was an offence to the world, is no marvel. It was so then, it is so now, and it

will be so to the end. But our Lord never, in any one instance, gave
NEEDLESS offence. His heart was too tender, His disposition too
kind, His nature too holy, maliciously and thoughtlessly to wound
the feelings or offend the 'innocent sentiments' of others. Maligned
by His enemies, misunderstood and neglected by His friends, yet
on no occasion did He retort, revile, or wound; but, with the harm-
lessness of the dove and the innocence of the lamb. He opened not
His mouth. Let us learn of Him in this holy feature of His character, study it closely, and imitate it faithfully.

A desire to avoid offence does not demand a compromise of our
Christian faith or profession. On no occasion did it in the life of Jesus. When He might have avoided a snare, or warded off a thrust,
or escaped a wound by concession, conciliation, or compromise,
He stood firm to His own truth and His Father's honor, unswerv-
ing and unswerved—and yet the *"sword"* with which He fenced
and foiled His foes was, *"bathed in heaven"* (Isa. 34:5). Thus, O
my soul! learn of Him. Let this be your guiding precept, as it was
Christ's, *"speaking the truth in love."* Offences will come. For,
since *"the offence of the cross is not ceased,"* we cannot main-
tain its great distinctive and essential doctrines purely, faithfully,
manfully, and not evoke animosity against us; nor the hostility
and offence of the world.

And yet the Christian law, *"giving no offence, neither to the Jews,
nor to the Gentiles, nor to the Church of God,"* is unrepealed; and
the Christian precept, "that you may live pure and BLAMELESS
lives until Christ returns " is still binding upon all true followers
of the meek and harmless Savior. "The mind that was in Christ
Jesus," dwelling in us, will lead us to respect the convictions, to be
tender towards the feelings, and to be charitable towards the infirmities, and to honor the consciences of other Christians differ-
ing from us in things not essential to salvation. *"It is good neither
to eat flesh, nor to drink wine, nor anything whereby your brother
stumbles, or is offended, or is made weak."*

"Lest we should offend." What instructive words, O my soul, are
these! How much evil in the world, dissension in the Christian
Church, and alienation in families would be avoided and averted
were the holy precept taught in these words of Jesus more fully
observed. Let us, then, pray and watch against every least violation. Let us be careful of our words, our motives, and our actions,
lest, wounding and offending one of Christ's little ones, we offend
and wound Christ Himself. Oh never give needless cause of offence to a weak believer, to a conscientious Christian, to a tried,

tempted child of God—to one who, in his own way and sphere, is seeking to serve his Lord and Master. Let us deny ourselves any and every gratification, and allow any and every loss involving not disloyalty to Christ and compromise of His truth—rather than hurt the feelings, wound the conscience, or put a stumbling-block in the way of one who loves Jesus, and for whom the Savior died.

Oh, how seldom we remember, how faintly we recognize, the perfect ONENESS of Christ with His people! That it is utterly impossible to do an injury to, or confer a favor upon, a true believer in Jesus, and not be brought into personal contact with Jesus Himself—" *He that touches you touches the apple of my eye.*" "*Inasmuch as you have done it unto one of the least of these my brethren, you have done it unto me.*" Lord, help me more and more clearly to see *You* in Your saints; and in conferring upon them a kindness, or in inflicting on them an injury, to see *Jesus only!*

Consider Jesus—in Sickness *"He Himself took our infirmities, and bore our sicknesses."* —Matthew 8:17

How closely and tenderly is Jesus *one* with His Church! Take the subject of the present meditation as an illustration. There is not a chamber of pining sickness, nor a couch of suffering languor, at which His presence may not be experienced in all the divine power and human sympathy of His nature. The careful reader of His life must have been deeply impressed with the frequency with which His personal contact with bodily infirmity and disease is recorded, and with what promptness and skill He addressed Himself to the task of alleviation and cure. *"And He healed people who had every kind of sickness and disease."* And still His power and skill are needed, and still are the same. Into the shaded chamber of how many a sick one whom Jesus loves will these pages come, breathing, it is humbly prayed, the soothing fragrance of His Name around the restless pillow! *"He Himself took our infirmities, and bore our sicknesses."* Let us consider IN WHAT WAY Jesus did this.

He bore our sicknesses WHEN HE BORE OUR SINS. Sin is the prolific source of all evil, and especially of all disease. This reflection embitters and intensifies the sufferings of the child of God. The thought that, perhaps, had it not been for some particular defection, some hidden declension of soul, some sin of omission or of commission, his Heavenly Father would not have not sent the discipline of sickness—is intensely painful to the heart that desires to please God in all things. But how consolatory the truth that, if we may trace all disease to sin as its original and primary cause, we may also trace all sin to the cross of Christ, where He atoned for it, unsealing in His own heart's blood a stream which has cleansed it all away. Oh, let this thought, my soul, soothe and comfort you—that in all your bodily suffering there is no condemnation, the atoning blood of Jesus having washed you whiter than snow, leaving you not the *cause,* but the *effects* only of your sin.

But, if sin is the originating cause of sickness, *love*—divine, everlasting, unchangeable love—is the immediate and proximate cause. That is a sweet expression in reference to Lazarus— *"He whom you LOVE is sick."* No physician can bring to your sick-bed a medicine so healing, a remedy so soothing, as this truth— *that your sickness originated with a Father's love*—love selecting the NATURE, love appointing the TIME, love grouping all the CIRCUMSTANCES of the affliction. If, Lord, I can but see that *Your love* kindled this burning fever, appointed these silent hours, this darkened room, this unrefreshed bed, these quivering nerves, this throbbing head, this fluttering heart—"may Your will, not mine, be done."

Jesus bears our sickness in the grace and sympathy by which He enables *us,* uncomplainingly and submissively, to bear it. Oh, what a hallowed sanctuary is often the sickroom of a child of God! What divine presence is there felt, what glorious manifestations of the Savior are there made, what holy lessons are there learned, what heavenly prospects are there unveiled! Jesus is there, and thus makes it all that it is.

Be not hasty in judging of the state of your soul in sickness. Mind and body reciprocally and powerfully act upon each other. A diseased body will often impart its morbid complexion to a healthy soul; and, looking away from Jesus, will fill it with doubt, darkness, and despondency. It is what *Christ* is, and not what *you* are, that is to fill you with peace, joy, and hope.

Cheer up, my soul! this long, this painful sickness is not unto death, but that God may be glorified. When He has tried you, you shall emerge from this fire all the holier, and more Christ-like— rising from your couch and going forth from your sick-room, *"as a bridegroom coming out of his chamber, rejoicing as a strong man to run a race."* And thus by the *sanctifying discipline of sickness*, your covenant God and Savior is but preparing you to dwell in that happy land, the inhabitants of which shall no more say, "I am sick."

Consider Jesus—in the Anticipation of Death *"Father, save Me from this hour."*—John 12:27

There were some expressions of feeling in our Lord's life which can only be accounted for on the ground of His perfect *humanity*. Such, for example, as His apparent shrinking from suffering and death. And this, in its turn, can only find a solution in the fact that, He was not suffering as a common sufferer, but as the Sin-Bearer of His Church. We read of martyrs going to the stake displaying, apparently, much more fortitude than Jesus did in view of His death. The reason is obvious. In the case of the Christian martyr there was no burden of sin, no mental anguish increasing the tortures through which they passed to glory. The sense of God's forgiving love, and of acceptance in Christ, transformed the fiery chariot in which they ascended to heaven into a 'chariot of love'.

But the case of our Lord Jesus was essentially and totally different. His holy soul was suffering for the sins of His Church, and this was the cause of the shrinking and the cry in the garden of Gethsemane— *"If it is possible, let this cup pass from me."* He bore in His sufferings the burden of their *sins,* while they in theirs bore only the burden of His *love.* But what comfort springs from this consideration of Jesus *shrinking* from suffering and death, to those who are expecting the near approach of the hour of their dissolution!

Consider Jesus as having Himself TASTED death. What a comfort is this fact!

He knows what death really is. He tasted its bitterness, was pierced by its dart, felt its sting, and at length succumbed to the foe. He *died!* Thus, He can enter into your expectancy, fear, and shrinking, in view of this terrible crisis of your being, as no being on earth, or even in heaven, can. The glorified spirits look *back* upon death, but you are looking *forward* to death, and in its solemn anticipation there is but One Being in the universe who can deliver you from its bondage and its fear, That being is—JESUS.

But Jesus not only died, but, in dying, He OVERCAME and ABOLISHED death. It is no longer in the experience of the believer in the Lord Jesus death to die. Jesus has, in a sense, so annihilated death, so entirely absorbing it in His own Essential life, that He has declared; *"If a man keeps my saying, he shall not SEE death."* What an entire abolishment of death, must that be when a dying believer shall *not see death!* Yes, O my soul! looking in simple faith to your Savior, you shall see JESUS ONLY in that solemn moment. So entirely will He fill the whole scope of your vision, that death will be an invisible object—the pale messenger entirely hidden from your view by the personal sufficiency, beauty, and presence of Jesus. Glorious Savior! veiling the foe so long and so painfully dreaded, my dying eye will see You only—death's illustrious Victim, yet death's triumphant Conqueror.

Be not, then, O my soul! distressed in the prospect of your departure. Christ has come to *"deliver those who, through fear of death, were all their lifetime subject to bondage."* Alas! through lack of faith in Jesus, we suffer a thousand deaths in anticipation, while in reality we shall not suffer one! *"Those who SLEEP in Jesus"* is the epitaph which the Holy Spirit inscribes over the dust of every believer in Him. Away, then, with your fears, O my soul! Learn to die daily to sin, to self, to the world; and then from the valley of the shadow of death will ascend, as you pass down, the triumphant shout, *"Thanks be unto God, who gives me the victory through our Lord Jesus Christ."*

O You! from whose belt hang the keys of Hades and of death; *go ahead of* the "last enemy" with Your grace, *accompany* him with Your presence, and *follow* him with Your power; then shall I fear no evil, but fall asleep in Your arms and wake up in Your likeness.

"It is not death when souls depart,

If You depart not from the soul."

Consider Jesus—in Intercessory Prayer

"I pray for them."—John 17:9

There is no part of Christ's Priestly office more soothing to the sick, tried, and suffering believer, than His intercessory supplication on their behalf. To know that we are borne upon the prayerful hearts of our fellow-Christians, in times when providences are trying, and our hearts are breaking, is unspeakably soothing. How much more so is the thought that Jesus, our merciful High Priest, Friend and Brother born for adversity, is praying for us in heaven—our names worn upon His heart, our woes and needs, sins and sorrows entwined with His prayers before the throne; that, His intercession for us is not a *past*, nor even an *anticipatory* intercession alone; but, that it is a *present* intercession, an intercession moment by moment, "NOW appearing in the presence of God for us."

O sweet thought that, when some new trial comes, and some dark cloud lowers, and some bitter sorrow crushes; at *that very* moment *Jesus is praying for us*, asking His Father on our behalf the strength that will support; the grace that will sanctify; the love, comfort, and precious promise applied by the Spirit, that will calm, soothe, and sustain us. Thus consider Him.

Intercessory prayer for others is one of our most spiritual and richest privileges. *"Pray one for another." "Praying for all the saints,"* is the divine and apostolic precept constantly enforced, and by arguments the most persuasive and touching. How many of the Lord's tried ones, through bodily pain, or mental depression, or crushing sorrow, *cannot pray for themselves!*

What a privilege to pray for them, to be "God's remembrancers" on their behalf, to imitate Jesus, and intercede for them *outside* the veil, while *He* intercedes for them *within* the veil! Thus, intercessory prayer on earth, and intercessory prayer in heaven, will envelop them as with a cloud of incense, and the tried saint will be upheld, and the weak strengthened, and the tempted shielded, and the sorrowing comforted, and the sick soothed, and the dying one supported and cheered, as he passes down the valley, homeward to be forever with the Lord.

For the use of those who visit the sick and the dying, the following PRAYER for one who appears to be approaching the eternal world is affectionately suggested—

"O Father of mercies, God of all comfort, our only help in time of need, we fly unto You for support on behalf of this sick person lying under Your hand, in great suffering and weakness of body. Look graciously upon him, O Lord; and the more the outward man decays, strengthen him, we beseech You, so much the more continually with Your grace in the inner man. Give him sincere repentance for all the errors of his past life, and true faith in the Lord Jesus Christ, that, washed in His atoning blood, which cleanses from all sin, he may have peace with God before he goes hence and be seen no more . We know, O Lord, that there is nothing impossible with You, and that, You can raise him up as from the grave, and prolong his life; yet, if it be Your will that he should die, so fit and prepare him for the solemn change by the regenerating grace of Your Spirit, and simple reliance upon the Savior of sinners, that his soul may have an abundant entrance into Your everlasting kingdom, through the sole merits and mediation of Jesus Christ our Lord, to whom, in union with Yourself, O Father, and with You, O Holy Spirit, be all honor and glory, world without end. Amen."

Offering up by that dying couch and in that solemn moment, this prayer in faith of the Divine assurance, that, *"He is able also to save them to the uttermost that come unto God by Him, seeing He ever lives to make intercession for them,"* we may humbly hope that, at the evening time it shall be light; and that, at the last moment, the brand shall be plucked from the burning, and free grace wear the crown.

Consider Jesus—In Bereavement *"Jesus wept."*—John 6:35

With what baptism of suffering was not Jesus baptized? What cup of sorrow did not He drink? Well may He ask, *"Are you able to drink of the cup that I shall drink of, and to be baptized with the baptism that I am baptized with?"*

"Yes, Lord," every believing saint may reply, "by Your grace I AM ABLE; for, while without You I can do nothing, with You strengthening me I can do all things." Jesus replies, "You shall, indeed, drink of my cup, and be baptized with the baptism that I am baptized with; for all My members shall be conformed to Me, their Head." "Dear Lord," responds the believing soul, "if affliction, temptation, and sorrow but mold me into Your image, and conform me to Your life, do with me as seems good in Your sight."

There are few sorrows more bitter and more keenly felt, than *the sorrow of bereavement.* Jesus knew what this sorrow was; let us consider Him in this light.

Are you bereaved? so was Jesus. When the wondrous words were written on which this meditation is founded, He was weeping at the grave of the friend He deeply, tenderly loved, and now as tenderly and deeply mourned. Baptized with your present baptism of woe, drinking your present cup of grief, He knows your sorrow, can fathom with His love its depths, soothe with His sympathy its anguish, and enter into all the intricate and delicate network of the loss and loneliness it entails. "Jesus wept."

And still in compassionate sympathy He weeps with those who weep. How truly human was the heart, and Divine the arm, of Jesus. With the one He moistened the grave with tears, and with the other He unclosed its doors and set its captive free. Both these natures—the Divine and the human—encompass you in your present bereavement. You need both, and both you have. The exercise of His DIVINE POWER in *resurrection* He may reserve for the moment when *"those who sleep in Jesus will God bring with Him; when the Lord Himself shall descend from heaven with a shout, with the voice of the archangel, and with the trumpet of God: and the dead in Christ shall rise first."*

But the outflow of His HUMAN SYMPATHY shall be *now*, tear mingling with tear, sigh responding to sigh, in this dark hour of your calamity.

My soul! let your first, your great desire be—not that your wound may be stanched, or your grief soothed, but that your God may be glorified in the fires; that henceforth your smitten and grieved heart may enshrine and enthrone Jesus, as the object of its single homage, and as the sovereign of its supreme rule. Has your God written you a *widow?* —then will He be to you the widow's God. Has He made you an *orphan?* —in Him the fatherless finds mercy. Has He by this visitation of death broken a supporting staff, dried a spring of affection, severed a source of supply, put out the lights of life one by one?—fear not! you shall now lean upon His arm, repose upon His heart, live upon His resources, and walk in His light. Thus learning by sweet, though painful experience, that the Lord never removes one blessing but to replace it with a greater; never seals up one spring of happiness but to unseal a deeper one. Then, let your bereaved heart exclaim— *"Whom have I in heaven but You, and who is there on earth that I desire besides You?"* All are not gone! Your God may have removed one by one of earth's sweet treasures; but He will never take Himself from you. Death may rob you of all but Christ.

"Launched on the tide of God's eternal love,
His ark beneath you, and His light above,
What can you fear? Be still, my soul, be still!
Your God has never left you—never will."
Consider Jesus—as Receiving Sinners
"This man receives sinners!"—Luke 15:2

Nothing gave greater offence to the scribes and Pharisees than the divine mission of Jesus to save sinners. No greater and more virulent accusation could they allege against Him, than that, He extended His compassionate regards to the vile and the wretched, admitting the most flagrant offenders to His mercy, and inviting the most notorious sinners to His fellowship. And yet this, His greatest reproach, was His highest honor. Pluck this jewel from His mediatorial crown, and it has lost its costliest gem. Extract this note from the "joyful sound," and you have hushed its sweetest melody. Remove this object of His mission from His coming, and you have reduced His incarnation, sufferings, and death to a gigantic waste.

Oh, with what glory does the fact that, *"This man receives sinners,"* invest the Son of God! How should our hearts glow with gratitude, praise, and love! If the individual who makes two blades of grass to grow where only one grew before, is regarded as a public benefactor; if we deck the person of him who, at the risk of his own, saves the life of another, what shall we feel towards the Son of God who, in the plenitude of His compassion and love, bowed the heavens, and came down to save countless myriads of our race from the "bitter pains of eternal death"!

Yes, "He receives sinners." He receives them *as sinners*—lost, undone, self- destroyed sinners—sinners too vile and too helpless to save themselves—who, if He does not save them, never can be saved. He receives sinners of all conditions and of every hue, of every depth of guilt and character of crime. Oh, if there were a sinner out-sinning all sinners—every sin tainting, every crime attaching to him—an abandoned profligate, an unbelieving scorner, a reviling blasphemer, a red-handed murderer, a profane infidel, a daring atheist, a moral parricide whose transgressions have broken a mother's heart and bowed a father's gray hairs in sorrow to the grave—sins as scarlet and red as crimson—as a cloud for darkness, and as the sands on the sea shore for multitude—if, I say, there be such a one whom He *would not* save, and *could not* save, then would there be silence in heaven and exultation in hell at the announcement that Jesus Christ had ceased to save to the uttermost bounds of sin and guilt all who, in penitence and faith, came to God through Him.

It follows, then, that, receiving them just as they are, He receives them *freely,* apart from all fitness or worthiness, of their own. *"By grace are you saved."*

"Being justified freely by His grace through the redemption that is in Christ Jesus." "Believe in the Lord Jesus Christ, and you shall be saved." What a joyful sound! Come, then, O my soul, to Jesus, without hesitation or delay.

> "Just as I am I and waiting not
> To rid my soul of one dark blot;
> To Him whose blood can cleanse each spot,
> O Lamb of God, I come."

Assured of the fact that you yourself have come to Jesus and are saved, be it your aim to bring others to Him, that they may be saved too. Oh, live and labor, if need be, suffer and die for Him, whose greatest glory is, that He receives and saves sinners, who has received and saved *you!*

"He receives sinners." Hear it, you that are afar off, wandering in ignorance and sin. Hear it, you who, amid the tortures of a guilt-oppressed conscience, are inquiring, "What must I do to obtain mercy and forgiveness?" Hear it, you who once walked in the way of holiness, but have turned aside to sin and folly. Hear it, you who

are resigning yourselves to dark despair, tempted to terminate a present misery by the self-infliction of a future, a more fearful and interminable one. Oh, hear it, all you poor and wretched, you humble and penitent, you broken-hearted and burdened— *"This man receives sinners, and eats with them."* "Come unto me, all you that labor and are heavy laden, and I will give you rest."

Consider Jesus—in His Atoning Blood "The blood of Jesus, His Son, cleanses us from every sin." 1 John 1:7

The blood of Jesus is everything. It is the *central* doctrine of our faith, the present and eternal life of our souls. There is no pardon, no salvation, no heaven but *by blood*—the blood of the Lord Jesus. Were we to relinquish every other revealed truth, and concentrate upon this one our supreme and lasting study, resolving all our knowledge of the Bible into an 'experimental and personal acquaintance' with ATONING BLOOD—as, like a purple thread, it runs from Genesis to Revelation, it would not be a too exaggerated view of this vital and momentous subject. The blood is everything to us—it is everything to God. He provided it, is satisfied with it, beholds it, and when He sees it on the soul, that soul becomes a living and a lovely soul in His sight. May our meditation on atoning blood exalt our views of its dignity, increase in us its power, and endear to our hearts the preciousness of Him who shed it!

The blood of Jesus is DIVINE. It is the blood of God's Son, the God-man Christ Jesus. In this consists its sovereign virtue. The Divine nature of Christ rendered His obedience and death an offering and a sacrifice to God of a sweet-smelling savor.

The blood of Jesus is ATONING. It was shed for sin, it has made to Divine justice a full satisfaction for sin, it puts away sin. Is sin your burden, O my soul? Is it for your sins you do moan and weep, and are cast down? Behold, the sin-atoning blood of Jesus; believe, and weep no more. Here is that before which not a sin can stand.

The blood of Jesus is CLEANSING. It "cleanses us." Oh, this is what you do so deeply need, my soul! Sin-forgiving, guilt-removing, heart-cleansing, conscience-purifying blood. All this is the blood of Jesus to you. Wash in it, and you shall be whiter than snow. *"He that is washed is clean, every whit."*

And mark the tense of the wonderful words on which this meditation is based—it is the *present* tense. The blood *"cleanses."* It *has* cleansed, it *will*

cleanse, but, as touching our daily walk as believers in Jesus, we have to do with its *present* cleansing. In our Christian travel through a sinful world the feet are apt to slide, prone to wander, and are constantly contracting fresh defilement, needing the *daily washing* in the blood. What a sweet thought, O my soul! that the fountain is *open*, and the blood *cleanses*, even *now* cleanses us, from all sin.

The blood of Jesus SPEAKS. "The blood of Christ that *speaks.*" Oh, what a voice has the blood of Jesus! What sweetness and majesty, what gentleness and power! It speaks, and the troubled conscience is at rest; it speaks, and the broken heart is healed; it speaks, and the tormenting doubt is hushed; it speaks, and the trembling fear is quelled. It speaks, also, within the veil. The voice of Jesus' blood is heard in glory, sweeter and louder than the voices of all the minstrels round about the throne. My soul, the voice of Jesus' blood pleads louder for you in heaven, than all your sins can plead against you on earth.

It is *sprinkled* blood—that is, APPLIED blood. Therefore it is called, *"the blood of sprinkling."* The blood of Jesus practically will not avail us unless applied to the conscience, just as the blood of the Paschal lamb had availed nothing to the Israelite, when the first-born of Egypt was slain, had it not been sprinkled upon his house. And so God said, *"When I SEE the BLOOD, I will pass over you."* O my soul! look well to this. Why is it that you are so doubting and fearful? Why are you not walking in a full sense of your pardon and acceptance in JESUS—basking in the sunshine of a present and assured salvation? Is it not because you are stopping short of the *applied* blood? Oh, come to the blood, the blood of sprinkling! Keep no guilt upon your conscience, no anguish for uncleansed sin in your heart; but wash daily in the precious blood of Christ, which cleanses from ALL sin.

Consider Jesus—in the Power of His Resurrection *"That I may know him, and the power of his resurrection "*—Phil. 3:10

Is there not some danger of lingering too exclusively at the *cross,* to the exclusion of the *grave* of Jesus? In other words, do we give the subject of Christ's RESURRECTION that place in our faith and meditation which we give to His Death, and which God gives it in the great scheme of our salvation? Essential and precious as the atoning Death of Jesus is, it had availed us nothing apart from *His Resurrection.* We needed more than *death*—we needed *life!* We needed more than the bond presented by Divine justice, and *paid*—we needed the seal of its acceptance on the part of God. This was given when God raised up Jesus from the dead, *"who was delivered for our offences, and was raised again for our justification."*

Christ's Resurrection from the grave by the power of God was the Father's attestation to the completeness of the Son's work, and His public acknowledgment of its acceptance. Thus the Resurrection of Christ is to us what a legal acknowledgment is at the hands of a creditor whose claim has been met, whose bond is cancelled. The believing soul sees in the emptied tomb of Jesus the evidence and the acknowledgment of his full discharge from all the demands of Law and all the threatenings of justice. Now, it is the *power* of this truth in our souls that more immediately concerns us. The Resurrection of Jesus is an accomplished fact—what we want to experience is, *His Resurrection-life in our heart.* This was Paul's prayer— *"That I may know Christ, and the POWER of His Resurrection."*

We first feel this when we realize our mystical union with Jesus. There can be no experience of the power of anything apart from a personal contact with it. Let us first settle the question, "Am I one with Christ?" Have I a vital and spiritual union with the Savior? If so, then I am risen with Him, as the apostle says— *"If you be risen with Christ."* O my soul, consider into what an exalted and blessed state your union with Christ places you, making you, through free and sovereign grace, a partaker of all that He was, of all that He now is, and of all that He will be when He comes with all His saints in majesty and glory.

By the power of Christ's Resurrection, we enter into a new, or *resurrection-life—"Quickened together with Him."* Our blessed Lord, when He rose from the dead, rose with a new-born life. Leaving in the tomb the grave-clothes—the napkin and the shroud—He came back clad with His resurrection robes— a new and wondrous life! Of this resurrection-life all are partakers who know the POWER of His Resurrection.

O my soul, fear not, then, that anything shall ever separate you from Christ. This cannot be, since your spiritual life is bound up and hidden with the Resurrection-life of Jesus.

The power of Jesus' Resurrection is experienced by us when by it we rise above earth, and *"seek those things which are above, where Christ sits on the right hand of God."* Has Jesus risen? Then we, also, must rise. As He left death and earth behind Him, so we, if we be risen with Him, "through faith of the operation of God, who raised Him from the dead," must rise superior to the deadly pomps and vanities of this poor world, and walk with God in "newness of life." Oh to feel the "power of His Resurrection," in a life dead to sin and the world, but living to holiness and God!

We wait to know yet more of the "power of Christ's Resurrection," when the trumpet of the Archangel shall sound, and the dead in Christ shall rise first. The slumber of the grave gently broken, the glorified spirit returns to its awakened dust—then both ascends into the air to meet the descending Lord. O blessed, glorious consummation of the power of Christ's Resurrection!

Consider Jesus—in His Second Appearing

"Looking for that blessed hope, the glorious appearing of the great God and our Savior Jesus Christ."—Titus 2:13

A Savior 'to come' has been the hope of the Church of God in every age and dispensation. The Old Testament saints looked for His coming to *save*; the saints of the New Testament look for His coming to *reign*—even *"The GLORIOUS appearing of the great God and our Savior Jesus Christ."* There are, in fact, *three* personal appearances of our Lord mentioned in the Scriptures. His first, when *"He APPEARED to put away sin by the sacrifice of Himself."* The second, *"Now to APPEAR in the presence of God forever."* The third, when *"He shall APPEAR the second time without sin* (that is, without a sin-offering) *unto salvation."* In each of these appearances of Jesus, my soul! you have a personal and precious interest. His *past* appearance was to save you, His *present* appearance is to intercede for you, His *future* appearance will be to glorify you.

And so Jesus is the "Alpha and Omega" of your salvation, from the *first* eternal throb of love towards you—if we may speak of a beginning of that which in reality had *no beginning*—to the *last* throb of love to you—if we may speak of the end of that which in reality has *no ending*. Thus, Christ is all and in all to you, the First and the Last, and, as good Romaine was used to express it, "and all that comes between." Let us consider Jesus in the light of the blessed hope, His glorious appearing, a befitting subject for the close of our daily meditation upon Him.

It will be a PERSONAL appearing. As He went up into heaven so will He *return—in person. "This SAME Jesus who was taken up from you into heaven, shall so come in like manner as you have seen him go into heaven."* So says God's Word, and so we believe. As His ascension was *personal,* so will be His coming again. This is a sweet thought, my soul, for you to dwell on. He will come not by His spirit, or by His angels—thus gathering His saints unto Him by *proxy*—but He will come for them *Himself.* It will be a *personal* appearing of the great God, our Savior.

It will, consequently, be a VISIBLE appearing of Jesus. "Behold, He comes with clouds, *and every eye shall see Him.*" "When He shall appear *we shall see Him as He is.*" Oh the thought of gazing upon His person, of beholding Him robed in majesty divine, and yet looking so human, so like His brethren, of whom He will now appear, more manifest than ever, the Elder Brother!

He will come WITH ALL HIS SAINTS. Those who sleep in Him will be raised, and those who are alive at His coming will be translated. Moses and Elijah, who appeared with Him in His transfiguration, were eminent representatives of these two conditions of the saints at His coming; Moses, representing those who died, and Elijah, those who will then be translated so that they shall not see death. *"The DEAD in Christ shall rise first: then we who are ALIVE and remain on the earth shall be caught up together with them in the clouds, to meet the Lord in the air."* Thus, whether living or dying in the Lord, we shall all meet again around the descending Person of Jesus, heart pulsating with heart, hand clasped in hand, one anthem sweetly chiming from every lip.

"Worthy is the Lamb, for He was slain for us."

This subject is eminently PRACTICAL. It makes Jesus more precious. How quicker beats the pulse and warmer throbs the heart of the bride anticipating the speedy return of her long absent lord! Blessed Jesus! You are the Bridegroom of Your Church, and the Beloved of my soul, and the thought of soon and forever beholding You makes my soul as the wings of Amminadab—unclasped, uplifted, and ready to fly!

O my soul! let not the coming of the Lord surprise you in a state of unregeneracy, unconverted and unprepared! None can meet Him with joy but those who are BORN AGAIN of the Spirit, washed in His blood, and clothed in His righteousness. Is this your assured condition? Then, happy are you!

Printed in the USA
CPSIA information can be obtained
at www.ICGtesting.com
LVHW011925040624
782280LV00014B/54